The Institutions
of Art

The Institutions
of Art

By Peter Bürger and
Christa Bürger

Translated by Loren Kruger

Introduction by Russell A. Berman

University of
Nebraska Press
Lincoln and
London

PN
53
B8
1992

© 1992 by the University of Nebraska Press
All rights reserved
Manufactured in the United States of America

Original publication information and copyright notices
for the essays that appear in this book can be found on
page 163.

The paper in this book meets the minimum require-
ments of American National Standard for Information
Sciences—Permanence of Paper for Printed Library
Materials, ANSI Z39.48–1984.

Library of Congress Cataloging-in-Publication Data
Bürger, Peter, 1936–
    The institutions of art / by Peter Bürger and Christa
Bürger ; translated by Loren Kruger ; introduction by
Russell A. Berman.
        p.   cm. — (Modern German culture and literature)
    Includes bibliographical references and index.
    ISBN 0-8032-1223-2
    1. Art and literature.   2. Literature—History and
criticism.   I. Bürger, Christa.   II. Title.   III. Series.
PN53.B8   1992
809—dc20   91-42754
                                                    CIP

Contents

In "The Institution of Art as a Category of the Sociology of Literature," the opening theoretical chapter of *The Institutions of Art*, Peter Bürger argues for the historicity of categories such as education, entertainment, and especially art and calls for the investigation of the historically differentiated function of the aesthetic norms and determining conditions that make up the institution of art in a particular period. In keeping with this injunction to respect the specificity of historically evolving institutions of art, I have envisaged this translation in part as a *Begriffsgeschichte*, or an account of concepts in the changing sociohistorical contexts of their use. Whereas German source texts cited in *The Institution of Art* appear to hide these changes behind individual words whose outward appearance may not immediately betray a shift in connotation, the corresponding English version can mark these shifts by changing the translation of key words.

This issue is nowhere more evident than in the changing meaning of terms representing the function of art in society. *Unterhaltung*, for example, shifts from the refined "conversation" that A. W. Schlegel associates with Boccaccio's aristocratic narrators and audience engaged in mutual distraction (chap. 6) to the light "entertainment" produced for an emerging middle-class reading public in the eighteenth century (chaps. 3, 4, and 6), and, in the course of the nineteenth century, the word merges with the phenomenon described by theorists of the culture industry as *Trivialliteratur*. In the context of the dissident intellectuals of eighteenth-century bourgeois society, this term is best translated literally to register these intellectuals' disdain for the books of conduct and moral tales that satisfied the bulk of the new reading public (chaps. 4 and 6; in the metadiscourse of present-day research, it is best rendered as "mass-market literature," which sheds the connotations of disdain to focus on the production and reception of these texts, without, however, predetermining the aesthetic or moral value of such practices.

The historical contestation of *Unterhaltung* has its counterpart in the dichotomy between moral instruction and general education. The early advocates for literature as autonomous art, such as Friedrich Schiller, Karl Philipp Moritz, and the Schlegel brothers, reject what they see as a degraded or trivialized *Unterhaltung* and an instrumentalized "schooling" (*Erziehung*) under the Enlightenment aegis of what Moritz dismisses as "the ruling idea of utility" (*herrschende Idee des Nützlichen*). Instead, they propose an aesthetic education (*ästhetische Erziehung*), "liberal education" (*freie Bildung*), or, conceived of simultaneously in universal and exclusionary terms, general "human development" (*menschliche Bildung*).

In translating the French aesthetic and critical texts from the same period cited primarily by Peter Bürger (especially in chaps. 2 and 3), I have followed essentially the same procedure. In most cases where Bürger cited the original French text or terminology, I have included the relevant quotation. In keeping with the historical specificity of the debates analyzed here, in which the protagonists were almost always men, I have left the singular masculine pronoun to mark the gendered character of public discourse in the period. Where present-day writers and general abstract arguments are at issue, I have used the plural where possible.

Moving from *Begriffsgeschichte* to Christa and Peter Bürger's own theoretical apparatus, I have followed common usage and current translations of texts by Karl Marx, Theodor Adorno, Herbert Marcuse, Hans Robert Jauss, and the like, modifying extant translations when necessary. When I depart from common usage, it is to highlight crucial points of difference between the Bürgers and those theorists whose positions are challenged in these essays. Thus, "content," the common translation of *Gehalt,* cannot be used to render the *Wirklichkeitsgehalt* (actuality) or the *geschichtliche Gehalt* (historical character) of the work of art, without reducing that historical or contemporary character to the very reductive concept of extractable content associated with reflection theory that the Bürgers' historical hermeneutics seeks to challenge. Similarly, the authors use *Wirkung* and *Wirkungsästhetik* (effect, or impact, and the aesthetics of impact) on the one hand, and *Rezeptionsästhetik* (aesthetics of reception) on the other, to distinguish their terms of analysis and their understanding of the functional determinants of reception and canonization in the institution of art both from a positivist investigation of measurable effects, or quantifiable impact, of a body of literature on a given public and from what they see as Jauss's essentially suprahistorical conception of the significant literary work as a unique event that breaks through a given horizon of aesthetic expectations, independent of the conditions shaping the institutionalization of art or the particular configuration of bourgeois society at specific historical moments (chaps. 1 and 3).

The Bürgers use the term *bürgerlich* to refer to a range of ideas from the specifically eighteenth century Enlightenment-bourgeois institution of art (as opposed to the institution of autonomous art that superseded it) to the more broadly defined "developed bourgeois society," which would necessarily cover the social context of both institutions as well as our own times. Except in those cases where *bürgerlich* clearly refers to the historically subordinate rather than hegemonic social group, as in the "middle-class readers" (*bürgerliche Leser*) targeted by the *Lesebuch für den Mittelstand* (chap. 4), I have generally translated *bürgerlich* as "bourgeois" so as to preserve the authors' emphasis on the epochal range and persistence of the social and political as well as cultural institutions which continue to sustain the hegemony of bourgeois culture under capitalism. *The Institutions of Art* thus falls within a tradition of literary scholarship that remains historical and materialist in orientation, however inflected by the aesthetic theory of Adorno and Marcuse and the hermeneutics of Jauss, among others. Even as it is accused of anachronism in the era of "post-Marxism," it reasserts the actuality of this tradition and the timeliness of this particular critical intervention in it.

I would like to thank Peter Hohendahl for giving me the opportunity to translate these essays, David Graver and Katie Trumpener for their comments on earlier drafts, Dawn Marlan for essential bibliographical work, and Stephanie Friedman for the index. Unless otherwise acknowledged, all translations of quotations are mine.

Introduction

Russell A. Berman

Despite several decades of an ongoing debate over the terms of literary theory, literary scholarship in the United States has apparently changed much less than is commonly imagined. Waves of methodological reform have come and gone, aesthetic and postaesthetic programs have been announced and forgotten, political agendas, hidden and otherwise, have swept through the universities and swept out again, but one centrally structuring feature of the profession has survived it all: in the end, the literary scholar still concentrates, by and large, on the intensive reading of individual texts, that is, on an interpretation, no matter what other name this activity may be given. Whether it is a close reading, in the manner of the old New Criticism (always maligned but rarely overcome), a deep reading of post-Freudian psychoanalytic criticism, or a thick reading of the anthropological new historicism, the American critic has proved unable to escape from the constitutive hermeneutic scene of examining single texts in relative isolation. This conservatism of the profession would, however, not necessarily be problematic if it did not conflict with the perhaps sole tenet shared by all the competing methodological schools, the insistence on the urgency of a posthermeneutic project and the importance of integrating extraliterary material into the discussion of literary texts. Even though they know better, scholars continue to uphold the enterprise of interpretation, as if there were an inherent structure of the literary material that could successfully resist all the theoretical calls-to-arms.

In order to demonstrate the dissatisfaction with the hermeneutic enterprise and its simultaneous tenacity, it is useful to review briefly some various routes that critics of interpretation have taken in recent years. The protean agenda of cultural studies, often borrowing from the work of Michel Foucault, has attempted to level the distance between aesthetic works and other cultural phenomena through the vehicle of discourse theory. Yet the wider historical vision that has ensued has bypassed, rather than solved, the problem of literary interpretation, ignoring the cultural fact of the stubborn staying power of the hermeneutic model, as well as the embarrassment of the privileged status accorded to artistic works within Foucault's oeuvre itself. Well-intentioned appeals to social relevance or revisionist politics may be successfully generating canons of great works by authors belonging to groups heretofore excluded from elite culture; needless to say, however, this is not an escape from hermeneutics but only its proliferation: more texts are accredited with the status of aesthetic singularity and therefore made available for interpretive scrutinization. The profession is consequently revitalized, pouncing on new material which it can process through its established machinery, geared to uncovering the meaning allegedly encoded within the work. This is the act of interpretation which, as Stanley Fish reassures us, "is the only game in town." [1]

In fact, it has been in the reader-response criticism of Fish and others, as well as in the reception theory of West German critics like Wolfgang Iser and Hans Robert Jauss that anxieties about the validity of hermeneutics were articulated most emphatically. The assumption of a stable meaning imputed to the literary work was undermined by the claim that the reader always participates in the production of the meaning. Given the multiplicity of readers, the possibility of plural meanings follows. Rather than leading to a historical inquiry into the assumptions underlying various readings, however, this insight has produced, at best, a retreat from objectivist truth-claims regarding any particular interpretation, which remains the unquestioned activity guaranteed by "the authority of interpretive communities." While the profession may have a history—Gerald Graff has come to similar results following different lines of argument—and its judgments may vary over time, judgment itself—the intensive reading of single works in relative isolation—appears to be impervious to history and consequently beyond critical examination. [2]

To understand that judgments take place within the context of the institution of the profession or the interpretive community is an important step beyond naive images of objective interpretation or critical isolation. It is, however, only a first step and does not yet explain why those counterfactual images retain a widespread currency. Indeed the academic celebration of deconstruction in recent years has meant the reassertion of precisely these images, especially the habitus of the oracular critic, whose authoritative utterances are immune to rational debate (denounced as just so much logocentrism and Western metaphysics) and who can bask in the auratic light of the infinitely mysterious text. Questions of history and politics, which New Criticism might have at least permitted, if only as extrinsic issues, have become simply bad taste, inappropriate to an exponential hermeneutics, inquiring into the question, the spirit, and the sacred, while skeptics are warded off with a dismissive *honi soit qui mal y pense.*[3] The critique of interpretation has not overcome interpretation but only generated a new and improved form of the same, and the hegemonic model of literary criticism remains the individual reading of the isolated text, the presumed separation of which from social processes is never examined consistently.

This is, after all, a rather odd model of literary criticism, certainly incompatible with the rejection of consciousness philosophy (with its implications for authorial intentionality and the status of meaning) as well as with semiotics and communication theory, which ought to have pushed literary studies toward an examination of larger societal structures and dynamics. More concretely, it is incompatible with the real character of literary activity at the end of the twentieth century. Authors may never have produced their texts in the romantic loneliness conventionally associated with poetic genius, but today they have even dropped the outdated pretense and understand how much they must confront the exigencies of the publishing industry, journalism, the commercial theater, and film. Indeed they probably understand these connections much better than literary scholars who are scrambling to don the romantic hand-me-downs of genius and loneliness, once reserved for authors and now recycled within the academy. So while scholars may be prudishly fearful of going beyond the text, even established authors like Joan Didion, Don DeLillo, and Norman Mailer, let alone more radical neo-avant-gardists like Laurie Anderson, generate texts impervious to academic hermeneutics because they wantonly disregard the pedantic separation of aesthetic form and political substance. Is this a blindness warranted by the authority of the interpretive community? It is certainly a consequence of the short-circuiting of reader-response theory through its dependence on the notion of the informed reader or the professional interpreter, as if the academic reading of the text were somehow always the most appropriate one, even though it is only the most privileged.[4] The road not taken by a reception theory that has been more concerned with the conventions of academic discourse than with any other sort of reception might have been to explore, more radically, other ways to read, or misread, popular reading habits, the problems of reading pedagogy in a stratified society, or the challenges of language and literature instruction in primary and secondary education.

The point is that the paradigm of hermeneutic criticism, which, despite all the methodological tempests, remains solidly in place in the university, systematically excludes, or at least marginalizes, a wide range of phenomena from literary study. The model of the isolated author inscribing a stable meaning into a singular text that is read by a fully competent and disinterested, isolated recipient for private edification is so extremely counterfactual that the viability of the illusion can itself be made the topic of a literary-sociological investigation. In the essays collected in this volume, Christa and Peter Bürger describe this assumption as indicative of a particular "institution" of literature, by which they mean the set of basic assumptions and norms in a given historical context that validate particular literary practices and denigrate others. In particular, the insistence on the auratic uniqueness of the text is symptomatic of the bourgeois institution of literature according to an aesthetic of autonomy, which was established in Western Europe—the essays here concentrate on France and Germany—about 1800 and, having weathered the early-twentieth-century attack of the historical avant-garde, remains very much in force.[5] The hermeneutic fixation of the contemporary academy therefore turns out to be part of a cultural framework that includes the romanticism of, say, Friedrich Schlegel, but not the older normative poetics of Nicolas Boileau or the enlightenment rationality of Denis Diderot and Gotthold Lessing. By historicizing this framework as a particular institution, the Bürgers hardly abolish it (although they each articulate criticisms of it in interestingly divergent ways), but they do open up its various functions to scrutiny. Instead of restricting literary studies to individual interpretations, the ramification of the Bürgers' work is to make this particular form of literary study itself a problem worthy of study, as well as the various sorts of issues that it excludes: the processes of literary production and reception and the institutional assumptions regarding the status of the work of art.

As a sociology of literature and art, the theory of institutions has to be separated from other comparable projects, notably an empirical sociology of literature, orthodox Marxist accounts, and particular aspects of the tradition of the Frankfurt School, from which it has emerged. The Bürgers' usage of the term "institution" should in no way be confused with a designation of empirical structures, such as the publishing industry, bookstores, writers' organizations, and reading societies. These are, to be sure, crucial aspects of the structuring of literary practices and their study can yield interesting results. Yet an empirical study that refrains from theoretical reflection is likely simply to repeat established theoretical positions in an unreflected manner and therefore remain within the assumptions of the hegemonic institution, which it is precisely the Bürgers' project to thematize. This relativization of empirical data should not, however, be confused with the marginalization of such information in New Criticism or its West German corollary, *werkimmanente Literaturkritik*. For the hermeneutic project, the overriding task of the critic or scholar is the interpretation of the text, understood as an autonomous work of art and therefore ultimately separate from any contextual substance; information regarding that context is therefore always at best of peripheral value. For the Bürgers, however, the context is crucial; indeed the work remains incomprehensible if the context is not taken into account: not, however, as an accumulation of data but as the contestation over the character of the institution.

It is, consequently, the struggle for the definition of the hegemonic program for literature which leaves marks within the works themselves. "The institution functions within the work, just as the work functions within the institution," writes Peter Bürger, thereby characterizing his own approach to Corneille's *Cid* and Christa Bürger's treatment of Kleist's *Erdbeben in Chile*. The former involves the competition between feudal and absolutist literary institutions, the latter the transition from an Enlightenment model to an aesthetics of autonomy, that is, the studies are centrally concerned with sociological formations even if they are not primarily empirical investigations of statistical data. For the theory of institutions simultaneously surpasses the antinomy of hermeneutics and positivism, which can be regarded as the reified separation of text and context. The Bürgers' work demonstrates that the polarization of those terms is itself a historical phenomenon, indicative of the fundamental assumption of literary autonomy within the bourgeois institution of art, the insistence that the work is self-contained, purposeless, self-referential, and ontologically separate from its surroundings. Rejecting that assumption, the Bürgers do not merely ignore it but make its plausibility and its consequences the topic of investigation.

The theory of institutions is a variant of neo-Marxist literary criticism, and while some of its features make it readily identifiable as such—the historical sequence of social formations, the adversarial stance toward bourgeois culture, the importance accorded to the socioeconomic standing of the writer, and so on—it is nevertheless incompatible with crucial aspects of orthodox Marxist criticism. That orthodox tradition has tended to include two functions (the relationship between which has always been tenuous). On the one hand, the paradigm of a reflective relationship between base and superstructure accorded to the work a cognitive status as a mirror of a social totality. On the other, the framing assertion of class struggle implicated the work in a particularist agenda as the vehicle of ideology. The former approach authorizes interpretive readings with regard to specific social meanings, that is, a Marxist version of hermeneutics, against which the general antihermeneutic arguments hold *mutatis mutandis*. The latter inquires into the political ramifications of literary representations within a conflicted society and its participation in what Louis Althusser has labeled the ideological state apparatus.[6] The Bürgers' accounts of literary history are, if anything, political, particularly with regard to the institutionalization of aesthetic autonomy, but they are political in more complicated ways, eschewing the mechanical connections implied by Althusser's concentration on the apparatus. For the institution plays a normative role that is larger than the empirical organizational functions of the apparatus, and it is the institution, rather than the political values carried by a particular work which is at stake for the Bürgers. Therefore the critique of the literature of bourgeois autonomy does not focus on the individual statements—the precise political claims inscribed as meaning in this or that work—but on the whole project of autonomization as the programmatic exclusion or concealment of politics. Of course, any flaunted denial of political significance is itself a political statement, but it simultaneously suppresses political rejoinders. In contrast, Christa Bürger can cite the model of the Enlightenment novel, which, despite some noticeably conservative loyalties, operates on the assumption that foregrounding political issues regarding social reform is the very point of literature and therefore elicits a public discussion on those issues. Autonomy aesthetics is viewed as indicative of a subsequent effort to truncate that public sphere.

Because an orthodox Marxist ideology criticism envisions works of art as necessarily expressive of specific class agendas at particular points in time, it will tend to generate historicist readings; the overall relationship between work and class is taken to be unproblematic. In contrast, the interest in the functional transformation of art in competing institutions is intended to problematize the status of autonomous art. Hence Peter Bürger's programmatic assertion that "the proposed category—institution of art—should be understood as a hermeneutic rather than a historical category. The point of introducing this category is to make possible a critique of the evolution of art in bourgeois society." While orthodox Marxism criticizes only the political substance of single works, the theory of institutions criticizes the general status of art and literature within bourgeois society, that is, the same autonomous status which prevents scholarly criticism from getting beyond the hermeneutic model of isolated interpretation. In other words, the privileging of the hermeneutic stance vis-à-vis the autonomous work—key features of the bourgeois institution of literature—is itself subjected to a hermeneutic inquiry that goes beyond accepting it as a historical phase, criticizing it instead with regard to constitutive features of bourgeois society: enlightenment, autonomy, and the public sphere. Autonomous literature is not denounced because it is a carrier of bourgeois values but because it suppresses the genuinely emancipatory aspects of bourgeois culture by depoliticizing the aesthetic discussion.

This dialectical judgment on the status of the work of art indicates the indebtedness of the theory of institutions to the legacy of the Frankfurt School. The essays in this volume take as their historical center the decades around 1800 because it is there that a symptomatic instance of the dialectic of enlightenment is played out. The Enlightenment model of art reduces reason to an instrumental rationality, but its corrective, autonomy aesthetics, defers emancipation indefinitely. While this historicophilosophical frame is effectively identical to the one that underlies the critical writings of Theodor Adorno, the model of criticism is extremely different. For Adorno pursues a Hegelian Marxist hermeneutics of individual works in which he ascertains an inscribed truth-value; indeed the autonomous work of art at its most hermetic becomes the last refuge of truth in an otherwise totally mediated and therefore totally false society.[7] The importance he ascribes to the work of art is therefore a corollary to a historical and political pessimism, arguably appropriate in the era of National Socialism, Stalinism, and the mass conformism of the United States to the culture industry. The Bürgers' theory of institutions, however, emerges after 1968 in a political context that allows for a historical relationship to classical Critical Theory as well as for some moderate optimism with regard to the possibilities of political contestation within the art world. While Adorno is certainly critical of the conservative implications of autonomy aesthetics, he locates in the autonomous work the residual enclave for an emancipatory politics in hibernation. For the Bürgers, autonomy is the perpetual alibi to exclude political considerations from art.

Shifting the discussion from the autonomous work to the institution of autonomy, the Bürgers abandon the consistent pessimism of Adorno's negative teleology and explore the internal differentiation of bourgeois society. On this point they approximate the concerns of Jürgen Habermas, especially with regard to his rearticulation of Max Weber's account of modernity as a separation of value spheres. Art attains a relative autonomy; that is, works are not judged immediately in terms of scientific accuracy or moral appropriateness and should therefore not be reduced fully to political statements or subsumed directly into a discursive formation of power. The point is to defend at least a limited zone of discussion and negotiation, separate both from economic interests and from administrative control. In this sense, the identification of the institution of art represents somewhat of a corollary to Habermas's concept of a public sphere.[8] However, the prevailing assumptions in the institution, that is, autonomy aesthetics, effectively cancel out the relative autonomy of art because of their subversion of any public discussion. Hence again the dialectical criticism implied by the institution theory: the autonomy model (of the work of art) undermines autonomy (of the recipient) by restricting considerations to aesthetic self-referentiality. The price bourgeois society exacts for artistic freedom is inconsequentiality, Auden's "For poetry makes nothing happen."[9]

Focusing on institutions rather than single works, the Bürgers relativize the hermeneutic model with its privileging of the isolated text as symptomatic of one particular institution. Clearly the "institution" is not the collection of material practices with regard to art and literature but rather an ideal-typical construct of expectations and values which, within a specific historical context, grant particular practices priority. Indeed at any point in time, various institutional models may coexist and compete, but— a Hegelian element in the argument—the suggestion is that one model will attain hegemony and generate pejorative judgments on other modes of writing, reading, and so on. Furthermore, the theory of institutions is lodged within a post-Marxist historicophilosophical frame, whereby an absolutist model of literature as a vehicle for the display of courtly power is supplanted by the Enlightenment model of pedagogy, which in turn gives way to the aesthetics of autonomy. In the United States, Peter Bürger is already known as the author of *The Theory of the Avant-garde*; the avant-garde movements of the early twentieth century play a pivotal role in his theory because dadaism, cubism, and constructivism are understood as the first consistent attack on the institution of autonomous art.[10] The vicissitudes of that attack and its mixed results are the topic of the earlier book. In this book, the Bürgers turn away from the investigation of a historical attempt to end bourgeois art and examine instead its origins. In addition to the particular insights they provide on a series of literary-historical topics from Corneille to Kleist, they elaborate a literary-sociological outline of the emergence of the expectations regarding literature—the institution—which still structure contemporary expectations, if not all contemporary practices. The ramification of the volume is therefore dialectical, for directing their attention to the beginnings of bourgeois assumptions regarding literature, the authors challenge contemporary scholarship to move beyond those assumptions or, failing that, at least to explain why it cannot.

Notes

1. Stanley Fish, "What Makes an Interpretation Acceptable," in *Is There a Text in This Class? The Authority of Interpretive Communities* (Cambridge, Mass.: Harvard University Press, 1980), 355.

2. Gerald Graff, *Professing Literature: An Institutional History* (Chicago: University of Chicago Press, 1987); cf. Peter Uwe Hohendahl, *Building a National Literature: The Case of Germany, 1830–1870*, trans. Renate Baron Franciscono (Ithaca: Cornell University Press, 1989), 4–13.

3. Cf. Jacques Derrida, "But, beyond . . . (Open Letter to Anne McClintock and Rob Nixon)," trans. Peggy Kamuf, in *"Race," Writing, and Difference*, ed. Henry Louis Gates, Jr. (Chicago: University of Chicago Press, 1986), 354–69.

4. Cf. Stanley Fish, "Literature in the Reader," in *Is There a Text in This Class?* 48.

5. The seminal discussion of "aura" is of course in Walter Benjamin, "The Work of Art in the Age of Mechanical Reproduction," in *Illuminations*, trans. Harry Zohn (New York: Schocken, 1969), pp. 217–52; for Benjamin's comments on literary scholarship, cf. his *Gesammelte Schriften*, vol. 3, ed. Hella Tiedemann-Bartels (Frankfurt, 1972), 191–93, 283–90.

6. Louis Althusser, "Ideology and Ideological State Apparatus," in *Lenin and Philosophy*, trans. Ben Brewster (London, 1971), 121–73.

7. See, for example, Theodor W. Adorno, "The Artist as Deputy," in *Notes to Literature*, vol. 1, trans. Shierry Nicholsen Weber (New York: Columbia University Press, 1991), 98–110.

8. Jürgen Habermas, *The Structural Transformation of the Public Sphere: An Inquiry into a Category of Bourgeois Society*, trans. Thomas Burger (Cambridge, Mass.: MIT Press, 1989).

9. W. H. Auden, "In Memory of W. B. Yeats," in *Collected Poems*, ed. Edward Mendelson (New York: Random House, 1976), 197.

10. Peter Bürger, *The Theory of the Avant-garde*, trans. Michael Shaw (Minneapolis: University of Minnesota Press, 1984).

Peter Bürger

1.

The Institution of Art as a Category of the Sociology of Literature

Toward a Theory of the Historical Transformation of the Social Function of Literature

Where Adorno (and, in a different sense, Lukács) was dedicated to interpreting the historical character [*Gehalt*] of individual works, an empirical sociology of literature has concerned itself with investigating the *impact* [*Wirkung*] of works of art. Adorno's critical target is this sociology of art, which is focused on impact that can presumably be grasped empirically:

> the effects of works of art, and of images of the imagination [*geistige Gebilde*] in general, are not absolute or final, nor can they be determined by recourse to the recipients. Effects depend rather on countless mechanisms of dissemination, social control and authority, and finally the social structure itself, within which the context of their impact can be constituted; also significant are the socially determined conscious and unconscious, on which the impact is exercised.[1]

The arguments which Adorno formulated address the central flaw in positivist sociology of art. It would nonetheless be no accident if his remarks were misunderstood as a fundamental rejection of empirical investigation.[2] For Adorno's challenge to the sociology of art offers no theoretical space for the inclusion of empirical investigation. To be sure, Adorno called for a sociology of art, which would link the analysis of works, the "structural and specific influence mechanisms" and "subjective responses susceptible to measurement," but he did not formulate a theory that might allow for the realization of such a link.[3] His aesthetic theory is a theory of the social character of the individual work, derived from its formal structure.

I have attempted on another occasion to show why Adorno and Lukács limit their investigation to grasping the social character of individual works and groups of works, without elaborating a theory of the function of art.[4] At issue here is the presupposed *identity,* based on the evolution of art in bourgeois society, of what Adorno calls "structural mechanisms of influence," and of what I term the "institution of art." A hermeneutic theory must take into account the conditions determining the possibility of articulating these mechanisms. This can happen only if the theory establishes its position on the evolution of its object of study. That is what I attempted to do for the "institution of art" in *Theory of the Avant-garde.* If the thesis presented in that book is right, that is, if the historical avant-garde movements attacked and thus made visible the autonomous status of art, then the end of the historical avant-garde movements enables the articulation of a sociology of art which encompasses art's autonomous status as the determining institutional condition of the production and reception of art. This claim is not based on subjective accounts of effects hypostasized as social facts (Silbermann), nor is it limited to the interpretation of the social character of individual works and groups of works (Adorno, Lukács). Instead, it attempts to determine the epochal limit conditions of literary production and reception. If a theory of the historical transformation of the social function of literature or art can be formulated, it ought likewise to be possible to link the immanent analysis of works with reception research in such a way that they illuminate each other and not merely present a marginal reception history of individual authors *alongside* the interpretation of individual works. In other words, our goal is to overcome the unproductive dichotomy between dialectic and positivistic sociology of literature, or, more precisely, to establish a terrain on which critical theorems can be tested with respect to historical material.

In the sociology of literature and art, the concept of the "institution of art" is occasionally employed to denote social formations [*gesellschaftliche Einrichtungen*] such as publishers, bookstores, theaters, and museums, which mediate between individual works and the public.[5] "Institution of art" will not be used in this sense here; the concept rather refers to the epochal functional determinants of art within the bounds of society. I will not contest the possibility of a sociology of instances of mediation; just as there is a sociology of law, so could one develop a sociology of theater. Only, this sort of empirical sociology of instances of mediation is not likely to illuminate the social function of art and its historical transformation. Adding investigations of individual instances cannot replace theoretical coordinates, which alone can form the basis for research on the social function of art.

The work of Thomas Neumann reveals the problems in an empirical investigation which is not connected to such a theory of historical trans-formation in the social function of art.[6] Neumann investigates the problem of the autonomization [*Autonomie-Setzung*] of artistic subjectivity, using Schiller as an example. But because he treats the problem in isolation and not in the context of its multiple social determinants, he risks treating Schiller's theoretical writings merely as texts documenting the stabilization of an autonomous artistic character and thus risks erasing their theoretical content. In his chosen mode of interpretation, Schiller's references to the social determinants of the "autonomizing" process of art and the artistic character are (mis)read merely as a strategy of justification. Despite this shortcoming, Neumann's work is significant because it is one of few at-tempts on the part of professional sociologists to track the problem of the autonomy of art (here, artistic subjectivity).

If we take the historicity of the category of art seriously, that is, if we assume that the evolution of categories is not independent of the object of investigation to which it refers, then suprahistorical definitions become problematic to the extent that they aim to be more than merely heuris-tic. A theory of the historical transformation of the institutionalization of art must therefore begin with a purely formal definition, so as not to hamper the research of historical changes with definitional stipulations. Acknowledging the fact that the collective designation of products of the imagination from very different fields of activity as "works of art" presup-poses a concept of art that emerges only in the eighteenth century, we can treat as the *institution of art* those notions about art (its functional deter-minants) which are generally valid in a society (or in individual classes or ranks). This formulation assumes that those functional determinants are linked to the material and ideational requirements of the works bearing them and that such determinants bear a definable relation to the *material conditions of the production and reception of art*. The differentiation of the functional determinants follows, mediated by aesthetic norms affecting *artistic material* on the producer's side and the establishment of attitudes of reception on the recipient's side.[7]

A theory of the historical transformation of the social function of art, which takes account of the historicity of the category, must take as its point of departure the most developed state of the object, that is, "art" as a fully differentiated social subsector [*gesellschaftlicher Teilbereich*], as it has unfolded in bourgeois society. We will therefore begin by looking primarily at the institution of art in bourgeois society. Only in the second instance will we address the question of the institutionalization of art in a prebourgeois social formation.

If, as I have suggested, the concept "institution of art" denotes the autonomous status that art assumes in bourgeois society, then my use of the singular also needs clarification.[8] The concept of art has been a common and comprehensive designation for poetry, music, fine art, and architecture since the end of the eighteenth century. "The various arts were let loose from their moorings to life, thought of as a connected whole . . . ; and this whole was set up as the realm of purposeless creation and disinterested pleasure against social life, which in turn appeared to be strictly organized according to definable goals for a future order."[9] Obviously this conceptual definition allows only for an extremely general approximation of the conception of art prevailing in bourgeois society. But it does point to a particular notion of art linked to a complex of modes of conduct (purposeless creation and disinterested pleasure). If this concept of art and its associated circumstances can be described as the institution of bourgeois society, two things are meant by this: first, the *historicity* of the concept; second, its *effective force* [*Wirkmächtigkeit*]. By *effective force,* I mean the shaping influence of an institutionalized understanding of art on the reproduction and reception of works. The fact that even the historical avant-garde's attack on art's autonomous status in bourgeois society admittedly disturbed it without destroying it speaks for the power of resistance of an institution that appears to exercise functions within bourgeois society which cannot be easily taken over by other institutions.[10]

The singular term "institution of art" highlights the hegemony of *one* conception of art in bourgeois society. This does not preempt the institutional claims of alternative conceptions of art (e.g., *art social* [social art] or *Junges Deutschland*'s [young Germany] conception of literature). Nevertheless, we may assume that the hegemony of the autonomous conception of art compels rival conceptions to define themselves against it. We should also guard against the liberalist illusion of any "free competition" between conceptions of art in developed bourgeois society. The predominance of *one* (autonomous) concept of art is demonstrated by the struggle against committed art which is waged on several fronts. Moreover, the resistance to a sociology of literature, which is not narrowly conceived as an auxiliary field of study but rather claims to grasp fully the character of individual works, can, as Kurt Wölfel remarks, be seen as an indicator of the domination of the concept of autonomy.[11]

At first glance, the concept of autonomy seems to denote only the relationship between art and society as a whole; a brief discussion of the genesis of the concept shows, however, that it entails a functional determination of art in bourgeois society. This concept not only emerges at the same time as the first formulations of a critique of instrumental reason, which Max Weber identified as the dominant principle of bourgeois society;[12] the first formulations of the idea of autonomy in the work of Karl Philipp Moritz and Friedrich Schiller also reveal that the autonomization of art responds to a characteristic experience for the intellectuals of the emergent bourgeois society, an experience which could later be described as alienation: "The ruling idea of *utility* has gradually repressed the noble and the beautiful—one contemplates even great sublime nature only with the eyes of a bureaucrat, and finds her appearance interesting only insofar as one calculates the sum of her products." So wrote Moritz in "Das Edelste in der Natur" (1786).[13] And, as is well known, Schiller grounded his theory of aesthetic education of individuals on a critique of the consequences of the historically necessary division of labor: "Eternally bound to a single small fragment of the whole, human beings imagine themselves only as fragments."[14] At issue here are not the distinctions between Moritz, who attributes imaginative elevation above reality to anyone independent of his social situation, and Schiller, who understands the effect of the division of labor as the maiming of the individuals. What is decisive in this context is the fact that, in the period in which the essential founding principles of the emergent bourgeois society (instrumental reason and the division of labor) become apparent, art is in turn understood as the single possible field in which the lost totality of humanity can be regained. Once religion in the course of the European Enlightenment lost its universal validity as the principle of reconciliation and after it had for centuries performed the double task of expressing a critique of society while rendering that critique without consequence, art took its place—at least for a class privileged by property and education. Art is supposed to restore the harmony of human character destroyed by daily life strictly organized in terms of instrumental reason.

> True art is not merely transient play, however; it is seriously concerned not merely to transport human beings into a momentary dream of freedom, but rather to make them really free, and to achieve this goal by awakening, exercising, and developing strength in them, to draw the sensuous world, which otherwise burdens us as raw material and weighs on us as a blind power, to an objective distance, to transform it into a free product of our imagination and thus to master the material through ideas.[15]

The contradictory character of the institution of art in bourgeois society becomes tangible here: the experience in the realm of ideas of the "freedom of the spirit [Gemüt] in the lively play of all its powers" is apostrophized as actual, without changing anything in the actual conditions of human life. The trouble that Schiller takes to demonstrate that art is not "empty play" or fleeting pleasure after which humanity must return to the "depressing narrowness" of the real world points to the precarious situation of art in bourgeois society. On the one hand, art is called upon to be the alternative to the real world, which it can be only if set up in total opposition to that world; on the other, it is precisely this isolation that puts art in danger of becoming "empty play." In other words, the opposition to life-praxis is the condition enabling art to perform its critical function, even as that condition prevents the critique from having any practical consequences.

This aporia reappears at several different moments of Schiller's theory. As H. Freier has shown, the political dilemma—"all improvement in the political realm ought to begin with the ennobling of character, but how can character be ennobled within a barbaric state?"[16]—recurs in the aesthetic realm, which ought to have offered a solution to the dilemma. For education by means of aesthetics presupposes recipients who are [already] capable of the kind of interaction with works of art that Schiller has in mind. Precisely this interaction is not possible for the majority of the population, because of actual living conditions and educational arrangements.[17] In other words, Schiller's generous concept of aesthetic education is ideological to the extent that it affirms the possibility of its realization, without being able to prove it rigorously. The rank that Schiller occupies as theoretician suggests that there is more in this aporia than a simple theoretical lack: it points instead to the contradictory institutionalization of art in bourgeois society. The fact that one of the most significant bourgeois theorists of aesthetics was not able to resolve the contradiction between the demand that art offer practical and consequential critique and the impossibility of responding to this demand leads us to conclude that art in bourgeois society is institutionalized as ideology in the strict sense of the word.[18] Insofar as art's critique of a society organized in terms of instrumental reason is institutionalized as illusory experience of harmony, while simultaneously checking the possibility of its realization, it is ideological, or—to use Marcuse's concept—affirmative.[19]

The idea that "false consciousness" could be anchored in an institution may seem strange at first glance. One could say, however, that critical sociology offers a similar instance in its conception of the state in late capitalist society as just such an institution, whose functioning depends on the continued concealment of its social function.[20] Claus Offe has thus argued convincingly that the state in late capitalist society can perform its function (securing the interests of capital) only if it at the same time uses social means to conceal this function. Nonetheless, Offe's argument seems to me to be still grounded in the assumption that the Enlightenment's influence on the functioning of an ideological institution also leads necessarily to its breakdown. That this consequence is not inevitable can be seen in the fact that the bourgeois institution of art has survived the development of mass reproduction as well as the avant-garde movement's attack which exposed the institution's mode of functioning.

Schiller's aesthetic theory can obviously not be simply equated with the ideology of art as institutionalized in bourgeois society. The point of the above reflections was to suggest the connection between the critique of alienation and the autonomous concept of art. We can follow this connection through the Romantic conception of art to aestheticism. At the center of Paul Valéry's critique of the everyday perspective is its orientation to utility—"the useful chases [away] the real" [l'utile chasse le réel].[21] He contrasts this perspective fixed on a prescribed goal with a pure (artistic) way of seeing; his argument thus bases itself on a concept of art according to which art and the modes of conduct associated with it stand in opposition to human life-praxis.

The problem of trivial or mass-market literature [Trivialliteratur] also suggests that it makes sense to proceed on the basis of the domination of

the institution of art in bourgeois society. An equivalent to what later became mass literature already existed in prebourgeois society (for example, the *bibliothèque bleue* in seventeenth- and eighteenth-century France),
although the idea of mass literature was not *a problem* for the culturally
dominant class of high absolutist society. It became a problem only in
the moment when bourgeois conceptions of life and the world began to
establish themselves. Only with the development of the bourgeois concept
of the universally human did the demand emerge for the general accessibility of literature, including high literature. The aesthetic of the Abbé
du Bos, which makes the notion of a universal emotion into the foundation of sensitivity toward works of art, may be seen as an early attempt
at a theoretical resolution of this new demand.[22] Toward the end of the
eighteenth century, Schiller addressed the difficulty facing the writer striving for popularity.[23] He must overcome the distance between the crowd
and the educated class in his art. Schiller thought this task could not be
achieved during his time, however. Art was in his view only for the educated. Schiller accuses the poet Gottfried August Bürger, who thought of
himself as a national-popular bard [*Volkssänger*], of accommodating himself to the "capacities of the crowd." The elevated charge that art be a
paradigm of reconciliation does not permit the fulfillment of the demand
for universal accessibility. Thus, for Schiller, exclusionary rules become
necessary to mark off art as a higher realm. The charge of triviality is
one such rule. The problems of mass-market literature and the elite consciousness of the artist arise as a result of these contradictory demands
confronting art—to be both guardian of a humanity that can no longer be
found in life-praxis and yet be available to all.

A further problem remains to be examined here: the instrumentalization of art. Nothing appears to contradict the idea that art is set up as
an autonomous institution in bourgeois society more than the fact that
works of art in this very society are pressed into service as instruments of
schooling [*Erziehung*] and socialization. We should remember, however,
that the differentiation of a social subsector for art does not presuppose its
isolation from society as a whole. Rather, the differentiation of subsectors
can take place only on the basis of a relatively developed social whole.
This differentiated social subsector, which functions according to its own
rules, still depends on the social whole, for which it undertakes particular
tasks. The concept of autonomy may, for some artists, be associated with
the idea of independence from society, but as we have seen in Schiller's

theory, the concept functions institutionally to mean emancipation from *immediate* demands for social application; this emancipation is, however, achieved so as to enable art to perform functions for society as a whole which are not (or no longer thoroughly) performed by other institutions. Art is institutionalized as autonomous to act as guardian of human emancipation in a society whose actual life processes do not allow its realization. The fact that art so conceived is put to service in the bourgeois education system does not contradict the concept of autonomy; in fact it demands this instrumentalization. The education of humanity is realized in the first place with the aid of works of art. The apparent contradiction between autonomous art and the instrumentalization of the work in the schooling process dissolves when we explain that works of art can be pressed into service as instruments of schooling precisely because of their autonomous status.[24]

As far as I know, only one approach in the discussion about the possibility of a sociology of art claims to examine the institutionalization of art in bourgeois society as a whole: the economic approach. Along the lines of Brecht's critique of the bourgeois concept of autonomy in his *Threepenny Lawsuit* [Dreigroschen-prozess], this approach argues that the work of art in bourgeois society is a commodity and, like every other commodity, is subject to the valorization interests of capital. We cannot examine in detail the problems associated with this theorem but must focus on examining to what extent this approach can make sense of the transformation of the social function of art. There is certainly no doubt that works of art are treated like commodities in bourgeois society, and there are certainly grounds for assuming that these modes of the dissemination of works of art are not merely external. The difficulty remains in trying to establish the extent to which this is true. Only if the commodity form's determination of the social function of works of art can be demonstrated would this approach represent an alternative to the one I have suggested here. That demonstration is unlikely. Starting from a juxtapostion of industrial labor and artistic labor, which emphasizes the discrepancies between them, Hannelore Schlaffer comes to the conclusion that the capitalist conditions of distribution, to which works of art are subject, do not intersect with the realm of their social function: "Since the marketing of art can be abstracted from their aesthetic specifics, a critique that is restricted to this distribution, has little of consequence to say about the function of art in present-day society."[25] One might object that the talk about "aesthetic specifics" restores the very ideology of "art" under investigation as a social institution; Schlaffer's critique is nonetheless right in arguing that the commodity character of works of art does not enable us to make sense of their function.

It would nonetheless be wrong to conclude that the problem articulated by the theorem of art as commodity is therefore irrelevant. At issue is the question of the connection between the institutional status of art and the material conditions of its production in a particular society. Gerhard Leithäuser has shown that the question of the degree to which art is subject to capitalist relations can also be relevant in the determination of autonomous art. He comes to the conclusion that there are two distinct levels of art's subjection to capitalist relations, formal and actual prescription: "Formal prescription essentially leaves the producer of art with control over artistic tools and thus also over an essential aspect of autonomy. Actual prescription by capitalist relations turns the artist into a proletarianized dependent employee, almost completely bereft of the conditions for autonomous artistic practice."[26] It is easy to see—and Leithaüser, too, understands the distinction between the two levels of the subjection of art to capital in this sense—that autonomous art remains at the stage of formal prescription ("progress" toward actual prescription would extinguish art as "art"), whereas the culture industry has reached the stage of actual prescription (its production is completely tied to the valorization of capital). The fact that the distinction between autonomous art and the culture industry is not merely subjectively imagined but, rather, corresponds to a precise economic situation makes clear that a theory of the historical transformation of the social function of art must examine the relationships between the epochal institutionalization of art and the material conditions of its production.

Thus far, we have examined the conception of the institution of art exclusively in the context of bourgeois society. The reason is its character as a *historical category*. In other words, the emergence of the institution of art, as well as its discernibility as institution, is determined by the evolution of art in bourgeois society. The insight that art is an institution in bourgeois society and that particular conceptions of art regulate the production and reception of individual works leads us to the question of the institutionalization of art in prebourgeois society. This question is difficult to pose because a concept of art, which is itself a product of historical processes, slips surreptitiously into its very formulation. "Art" in the modern sense of the word refers to those artistic practices loosened from moorings to real life.

If we want to investigate the institutionalization of literature, for instance, in a prebourgeois social formation, we would have to take care to avoid simply imposing subcategories and relations from autonomous art on this other literature. In other words, this investigation depends on a historical conception of the category "institution of art." It is not easy to work with a category that changes historically. For the reciprocal determination of subcategories and their relationships cannot be fixed for all time; rather, the elaboration of categorical terms is itself connected to the historical investigation of the subject.

If it is true that the presuppositions of the categories of historical-hermeneutic scholarship lie in the actual stage of evolution of the subject, then any isolated discussion of categories becomes problematic because it cannot but give the impression that the categories are autonomous. Strictly speaking, the evolution of categories should be seen in the context of the historical evolution of the notion of autonomy itself.[27] If we nonetheless attempt to develop "institution of art" as a general category (i.e., one that is not connected to a particular social formation), then the attempt takes the form of a historical construction that must remain abstract to the extent that the history of the social function of art is not yet written. Such a historical construction is not merely the anticipation of the results of individual research projects but the only possible guarantee that they do not get mired in a positivist fetishization of detail.

Our historical construction is limited to juxtaposing the institution of art in bourgeois society with the institutionalization(s) of literature in the feudal court of seventeenth-century France. This construction deliberately forgoes the explication of developmental tendencies so as to examine the connection between a social formation and a particular kind of institutionalization. The issue is above all to apply the insight about the historicity of the category "institution of art" to a practical research context, that is, to grasp the subcategories and their reciprocal relationships in their historical variability. For example, we have already shown that art functions as ideology in bourgeois society. This supposition need not apply to the institutionalization of literature in the feudal court of France. In contrast to bourgeois society, feudal society is defined by the principle of legitimately justified inequality. The nobility had particular privileges as a result of the simple fact that they were nobly born. A society in which the principle of legal inequality is institutionalized would not develop an ideology, even in the realm of art, for ideologies in the strict sense of the word evolved only on the basis of formal equal rights in bourgeois society. We can, rather, assume that artistic practices were separated from one another by boundaries between the ranks which determine social life. Indeed, the feudal court in seventeenth-century France displays several institutionalizations of literature, which are distinctly separate from one another and which are characterized sometimes by their economic base, sometimes by a specific bearer class, or by a more or less developed system of aesthetic norms which corresponds in a determinate way to social norms: specifically, popular, learned middle-class, and courtly institutionalizations of literature. The social significance of these various institutionalizations is exceptionally diverse and depends above all on the social standing of the bearer class.[28]

As we pursue this sketch of the distinctions between the bourgeois institution of art and the institutionalization of literature in feudal court society, we shall concentrate on classical courtly literature, because this literature in its canonized form serves as a point of reference for the later evolution of bourgeois literature. We have seen that art in developed bourgeois society becomes an institution cut off from life-praxis. In the feudal court, however, art is part of the nobility's life-praxis. We need think only of the importance of the salon or of the integration of art and life in the court festival. As a part of courtly representation and self-representation, art performs political functions; in immediate or mediated form, it serves the legitimation of absolute power. Even when art appears purposeless, as in the case of the courtly divertissement, it is nonetheless an instrument of a [monarchical] politics that robs the high nobility of their political power by tying them to ceremonial representation.[29]

It would nonetheless be wrong to attempt to define the difference between bourgeois and courtly institutions of art simply in terms of the opposition between heteronomy and autonomy. The historical dialectic is necessarily more complicated. The dependence of feudal court literature on social applications such as divertissement and monarchic representation contain at the same time a moment of liberation from other, especially from moral, obligations. This is clear from the intense attacks made by the church on literature and especially on theater. We should also note that moments of artistic autonomy are tied up with the suppression of courtly obligations; these moments later facilitate bourgeois literary criticism's subsequent understanding of courtly literature as though it were autonomous. To the degree that the concept of autonomy maintains a certain distance from the immediate goals of moral education, it also enabled the canonization of courtly literature in terms of eternal aesthetic value, even though this distance has evolved in courtly literature on completely different grounds (namely as a result of its orientation to an aristocratic ideal of life).

What distinguishes the material conditions of developed bourgeois society from those of prebourgeois social formations is the fact that the market becomes the decisive basis of artistic production—as opposed to the patronage which supports artistic production in feudal court society. Patronage establishes a relationship between patron and artist, which exists only as an individual case; as such, it corresponds to the personal relationship of dependence characteristic of feudal society. The type of dependence created by the market is rather different, namely, dependence on an anonymous public. The difference in the relationship of the artistic producer to his material basis suggests that the *relationship* of the material conditions of artistic production to general conceptions of art is also different. As long as the artistic producer's dependence on his patron is generally accepted, the tendency of production toward individual works which serve an individual producer will seem self-evident. In this situation we do not yet have an absolute creative subjectivity face to face with an unknown [mass] audience. Rather, artistic production is still understood as labor performed for the person who gives the commission, and the relations between producer and patron are as yet untouched by the opposition between the material basis of artistic production and the ideality of the artistic image. The conception of art as divertissement, which owes its existence to an aristocratic way of life, is accepted by artists as well because of the relationship of patronage; that is, patronage secures the social validity of a particular conception of art. Only with the rise of bourgeois society, when art is uncoupled from the realm of instrumental reason and thus autonomously institutionalized, do the material conditions of artistic production become something foreign to art as such. The relation of art to the material conditions of its production changes radically. The conception of art as divertissement in the feudal court referred thematically to the artistic producer's dependence on the lord patron; that is not the case with art in bourgeois society. Autonomous art in bourgeois society can relate only negatively to the material conditions of its production, since the autonomy of art was constituted initially in opposition to the realm of instrumental reason.

This difference has consequences for a socially grounded conception of artistic labor. Whereas the artist producing for a patron has a relatively unproblematic relationship to his own labor, the artist working under the conditions of bourgeois notions of art is compelled to conceal the traces of labor in the art object; that in its turn should manifest itself as a product of nature, since only in this form can it represent the obverse of the ruling principle of instrumental reason. Schiller thus spoke quite consistently of the manifestation of autonomy, not of the autonomous work of art. And Adorno has pointed out that "the autonomy of art can be conceived only if labor is concealed."[30] If we can now, at the end of the high bourgeois period, discuss artistic work as labor, then it is because the distance between art and life-praxis under aestheticism was radicalized by thoroughly erasing the social content of the individual work so as to exclude every possible confusion of artistic work with socially necessary labor.

It is one of the tricks of the dialectic of autonomy and heteronomy that this very radicalized claim for autonomy in art, which aestheticism formulates, coincides historically with the subjection of the aesthetic to the valorization interests of capital. It is precisely the experience of color, form, and sound, which is independent of social qualities, that is pressed into service for advertising and the emerging commodity aesthetic. Whereas moments of autonomy could emerge within the relations of dependence in courtly artistic production, art's total liberation from any social content tends to make it submit all the more to what it had rebelled against as autonomous work in bourgeois society: the rationalization [*Rationalität*] of capital.

A significant objection can be raised against the discussion of the institution of art thus far, that the categories (epochal functional determination of art and the material conditions of artistic production) touch on the limit conditions of artistic production and reception but remain nonetheless extrinsic to the individual work. One could add that, while the work of art may have to be measured against these preexisting limit conditions, it may not have any countereffect on them. In this case, we would have a portentous prejudgment, namely, the elimination of the dialectic between institution and individual work. In order to meet this danger, we must establish in the concept of the institution of art those categories which allow us to grasp that dialectic. We begin this task with the initial proposition: the institution functions within the work, just as the work functions within the institution.

The *concept of the norm*, like that of the artistic material, belongs to those categories which establish this mediation between institution and individual work. Whereas the institutionalized function of art and the material conditions of artistic production do determine the production and reception of the individual work, these conditions cannot be detected in the work. The situation is different in the case of both artistic material, which becomes part of the work after being shaped by the artist's subjectivity, and norms, which function as the social object of the literary work, while they shape its aesthetic character even as it resists. Aesthetic and social norms exist in a relationship of reciprocal tension, whose dialectic can be explicated only in point form here. At issue is not Mukarovsky's [structuralist] antinomy between "the norm's claim to be generally mandatory, without which there would be no norms, and its actual limitation and mutability" but, rather, the historicization of normative authority itself.[31]

In feudal court society, aesthetic norms are either immediately connected to social norms (one might think of *bienséance* [decorum] and the significance of rank) or they serve social interests indirectly (as in the dramatic unities, for example). Aesthetic norms mediate the character of the individual work by way of dominant social norms and so secure their relative conformity. This does not exclude the possibility of conflicts between the work of art and dominant notions of morality, as the clerical attack on Molière's *Tartuffe* and the difficulties surrounding the public performance of the play make clear. In the concept of the autonomous work of art, however, the concept of the norm is deliberately negated. The work is autonomous to the extent that it no longer obeys any rules imposed from without. The general concept of art characteristic of bourgeois society, which conceives of art in opposition to life-praxis, does not have a normative character; it contains no rules which are supposed to be followed in the production of a work. Instead, since the advent of Romantic criticism, the work of art is one that demands to be judged according to rules set by itself; this means that the work is no longer subject to institutionalized aesthetic norms.[32]

With the collapse of a mandatory aesthetic norm, the factor which had secured the relative conformity of the social character of the work in feudal court society also disappears. A work of art which is no longer regulated by any aesthetic (implicitly or explicitly socially determined) norm ought to be able to treat the realm of social norms freely as its object; that situation in turn would lead to a conflict that would endanger the existence of art. A society cultivates critique only insofar as its relative lack of consequences is guaranteed. This guarantee is established by the autonomous status of art in bourgeois society, which secures for art a certain realm of free play in the elaboration of social norms, but only at the cost of relative lack of consequence. Whereas literary criticism in feudal court society elaborates social norms, which are dealt with in the work of art, as such, the concept of autonomy makes possible their elaboration as a part of the work. As a result these norms are blunted, while the realm of free play for the work is expanded relative to prevailing norms. In other words, the mechanisms that help to secure the relative conformity of the work differ in each social formation. The autonomous status of art achieves in bourgeois society what was accomplished in feudal court society by the institutionalization of aesthetic norms. As in bourgeois society, the object of the work of art in feudal court society is the social norm. But since the work of art itself obeys aesthetic norms which are also social, the situation here does not get as far as the relationship of tension between individual work and social norms characteristic of bourgeois society. In other words, prior to the institutionalization of autonomous art the commitment problem does not exist. Only with the institutionalization of autonomous art does the politicization of the content of the work become problematic.

Another category that enables us to grasp the relationship between individual work and institution of art is the category of the artistic *material*. Let us recall the concept of material as established by [Hanns] Eisler and Adorno: as theorists of music they distinguish among various material realms (melody, harmonics, architechtonic forms such as the sonata), so as to work out the immanent dialectic of a kind of evolution in the musical material.[33] When a musical realm evolves, contradictions with other realms emerge, which become the engine of the *immanent evolution of the material*. This evolution may be called *immanent* because it does not correspond to any change in the social function of music. In other words, Eisler and Adorno start with the proposition that there is an "independent, musical-historical evolution" marked by changes in musical material.[34] This is an outline of one type of change in musical material, to be distinguished from another, which Adorno usually illustrates with the evolution of polyphony in the style of Bach into the courtly style of Bach's sons and the Mannheim School: "The courtly style of the early eighteenth century, which repressed Bach and the level of musical mastery that he achieved, cannot be explained according to musical logic, but with reference to consumption and to the requirements of a bourgeois consumer class."[35] In this case the change in the musical material is due not to an immanent dialectic but to the change in social conditions within which music is produced and received.

In the attempt to transfer the concept of artistic material from music to literature, we need to take account of the specificity of each medium. A concept of material concerned only with formal relationships would not address the subject matter of literature. However we designate the smallest unity of the literary work, what is certain is that it is semantically determined; it is the bearer of meaning. Thus motifs and themes ought to be considered alongside forms and genres as literary material.

Having clarified this essential distinction between musical and literary material, we have to ask how the concept of material fits into the theory of the institution of art. That can best be shown by juxtaposing this concept with the reception-aesthetic conception of the horizon of expectations. The horizon of expectations also includes moments of form and of content understood as a whole, since it depends on "the preunderstanding of genre on the basis of the form and thematics of hitherto known works and on the basis of the opposition between poetic and every-day language."[36] Nonetheless, the concept of material is different from that of the horizon of expectations in the following ways:

1. The horizon of expectations is not derived from the historical evolution of art but is introduced as a category with suprahistorical validity. The concept of material, however, takes account of its own emergence in a particular moment of the evolution of art in bourgeois society, namely, the moment in which the historical avant-garde enables the total liberation of motifs and procedures from the yoke of period conventions.

2. Reception aesthetics understands the literary work as an event, characterized by uniqueness and unpredictability.[37] As event, it breaks through a given horizon of expectations. The new literary work, which is supposed to be the engine of literary evolution, is thus removed from rational analysis. The concept of material, on the other hand, allows us to

analyze the new work as the rational engagement with prior material. The positive moment of the formalist impulse, the demand for rational analysis of literary technique, is here sublated, in the Hegelian sense of the word.

3. Reception aesthetics recognizes only an immanent literary evolution. The new work breaks through the public's horizon of expectation and so constitutes a new horizon of expectations. Extraliterary factors do not intervene in this process; at best, the literary work affects only the experience of the reader. But the concept of material allows us to distinguish between two types of literary evolution: one that is immanent and another that is occasioned in response to social demands. Paradoxically, the aesthetics of impact, which insists on the significance of the public for literature's process of evolution, reduces the recipient to an instance that merely completes what has already transpired in the field of production, whereas theorists of [artistic] material, who maintain the primacy of production over reception, establish the possibility of linking changes in the material to historically determined changes in the structure of the public.

A mere juxtaposition of alternatives (immanently vs. extrinsically determined material evolution) would be theoretically unsatisfying, if two completely different modes of evolution were proposed here. That is not the case, however. Both types of literary evolution give a central place to the labor of the art producer. This labor is guided in the first instance by *social demands,* which are made on producers; the concept of social demands seems to me more comprehensive than the requirements of the public. The impetus toward change in artistic material can follow from the producers' discovery of contradictions within previously available material, which they attempt to solve in the work of art. Those material changes elaborated by interpreters can be understood as the *intention of the work*— independently of the question whether these changes have been achieved consciously or unconsciously.[38]

Two examples follow which illustrate how this problem of the interconnection of institution and individual work might be solved.[39] Corneille's comedy can be understood as a significant reworking on the material of contemporary comedy and pastoral. Corneille's significance is so great that the dynamic of motifs in combination finally eliminates an essential element of comedy: the couple's happy reunion. This transformation of the material is so compelling that the plays move further and further away from the audience's entertainment demands, oriented as they were to the pleasure of tragicomedy. The young Corneille not only writes for an audience that does not yet exist, a bourgeois audience, but he also transforms the genre of comedy in such a way that it demands a different institutionalization of literature. Presumably literature should no longer entertain the public but ought to serve the process of the audience's self-realization; Corneillian comedy happens upon the type of institutionalization that it already presupposes. The works themselves point to a new institutionalization of literature, which does not yet correspondend to actual fact. Corneille responds to this institutional shift by ceasing his work on comedy. The transformation of tragicomic material thus reaches a point at which it comes up against the dominant institutionalization of literature which it cannot change; at this point it must be broken off.[40]

Whereas Corneille's early comedies can be understood as significant reworking of preexisting artistic material and, further, as an illustration of the possibility and limit of the immanent evolution of that material in feudal court society, the elaboration of classical French tragedy can be seen as an example of extreme determination of the material.[41] In this case the driving force of the change in dramatic material is the cultural politics of emergent absolutism. Particular social requirements (especially the need for a "great art" to correspond to Richelieu's *grand règne*) result in the introduction of rule-bound tragedy against the public's preference for the *tragicomédie irregulière*. The emergence of classical French tragedy cannot be explained according to the reception-aesthetic model in terms of a series of new works each of which explodes a given horizon of expectations. For it is not a new work that gives the impetus to a profound change in literary material in this case but, rather, the attack of the representatives of rule-bound tragedy, in consort with the central power of the emergent absolutist state, on the production and reception of the currently dominant tragicomic aesthetic. The presupposition defining the reception-aesthetic model of literary evolution—that no extraliterary factors intervene in the process of literary evolution—is valid only for the literary relations of developed bourgeois society—and then only in ideal-typical construction. An immanent literary evolution mediated by the recipient is conceivable only where art is established as an institution separate from life-praxis, although that would not exclude the social impact on individual works. In cases where art has to take over concrete social functions and is tied to life-praxis, as in feudal court society, there is no possibility of an immanent evolution. In cases where it might be proposed, it tends to be broken off, as the example of the young Corneille's comedy suggests.

The above reflections allow us to draw the following methodological conclusion: the *moment of the audience* [*Instanz Publikum*] must also be historicized. What changes in the course of social development are not merely attitudes of expectation and the social formation of the audience but also the significance of the audience as historical moment. In other words, whereas the prevailing present-day notion implies that it is the audience that changes and, with it, the attitude of expectation with respect to literature, leaving the relationship between literature and audience unchanged, it is this relationship that ought to be seen as historically variable. We ought to assume the unity of producer and receiver in artistic production in feudal court society. More important than the possibility granted the patron to have a direct impact on artistic production is the fact that the producers do not yet conceive of themselves as creative subjects independent (albeit ideologically) of society. The way in which Corneille broke off the attempt to create a bourgeois comedy and the fact that Racine gave up writing plays when Louis XIV made him *historiographe du roi* imply that the most important writers of the absolutist period of [French] court society did not yet see themselves as creative subjects. Where the producer has not yet been elevated to the self-consciousness of creative individuality, the public will also lack that independence which it gains in the context of bourgeois artistic production.

In bourgeois society, artistic production, now mediated by the market, separates producer from recipient. This dissociation becomes ideologized early on in the cult of genius, which reflects the new self-consciousness of the creative individual while concealing the actual social conditions of its emergence. The dissociation of producer and recipient has its bad sublation in mass-market literature, which negates both moments: the creative individuality of the producer is negated by the serially manufactured product; the distance, which maintains the recipient's integrity as against the work, is negated in the recipient's total identification with the work. Among other things, aestheticism is a response to the product's total accommodation, as is characteristic of mass-market literature, to "false," socially produced needs of recipients. Aestheticism seeks to realize the unity of producer and recipient without giving up the creative individual's claim for self-realization. In this context, the available audience shrinks to the dimensions of a small circle of connoisseurs, for whom the work's lack of impact becomes the measure of its value. Aestheticism can thus restore the unity of producer and recipient only if it reduces the potentially comprehensive audience to the dimensions of a circle with only a few members. Art is reduced to a private matter, threatening its authenticity, which is precisely what aestheticist artists were trying to rescue.

The avant-garde movements draw conclusions from this situation: for them, the recipient is either the sole endpoint of artistic action (as in dada happenings) or completely eliminated (as in *l'écriture automatique* [automatic writing], in which the individual text no longer has an addressee, strictly speaking). Hypostasization and elimination of the recipient are two sides of the same coin: the negation of the audience as an artistically meaningful entity. To be sure, the dada protest is focused entirely on effect, but it no longer envisages a public trained in literary example; rather, it takes the petit-bourgeois masses as the object of its theater of shock. Shock reduces the principle of effect to the simplest formula and thus also destroys the specificity of that effect. This reduction of effect to shock-effect negates the audience as a body able to enjoy and judge works of art. The abstract recipient takes its place. The negation of the public is the presupposition for the realization of the avant-garde intention to make art the organizing central principle of life. The break with an artistically competent audience does not, however, take art back into life but only generates the abstract recipient registering the shock. The autonomization theory of Russian formalism has conceptualized this stage in the evolution of art in bourgeois society. By treating the new principle of construction abstractly as the negation of the dominant principle, formalism offers a concept in literary scholarship which corresponds to the shock principle.

Finally, we should note some tentative consequences of the institution concept for practical research in the sociology of literature:

1. The separation between production and reception aesthetics, common enough in traditional literary scholarship, turns the dissociation of producers and recipients, dominant in late bourgeois society, into the foundation of research and so cuts off questions about the social conditions of this separation. The concept of the institution presupposes that epochal functional determination of art/literature apply equally to producers and recipients. In this way, the dissociation of producers and recipients can be researched as a historical phenomenon, and the

sublation of this opposition can be seen—pace the avant-garde—in a utopian perspective.

2. The separation between serious and mass-market literature is doubled by a corresponding separation in research. This is true for most ideological-critical studies of mass-market literature. Posed in the context of the institution concept, the question of the function of literature in society brings home the need to thematize the *connection* between serious and mass-market literature. The Russian Formalists have certainly discussed this connection but only within the limited problematic of the automatization theorem ("automatized" forms sink into mass-market literature, while other forms are appropriated by serious literature). In the context of the institution concept one would explain the appropriation of a noncanonical form not as the answer to "automatization" but, rather, as the producer's aesthetic and political attitude toward the dominant institution of art/literature. As long as we undertake separate research on serious literature on the one hand, and mass-market literature on the other, we run the risk of remaining within the dominant ideology of literature (as the discussion of kitsch has done).[42] If we want critically to illuminate this ideology, we must investigate the *process of the dichotomization of literature* in bourgeois society,[43] beginning with Adorno's acknowledgment: "Both [art and entertainment] carry the wounds of capitalism, both contain elements of change . . . , both are the sundered halves of the whole of freedom, which cannot nonetheless be made whole through their reassembly."[44]

3. Focusing literary research narrowly on "literarity" has meant that questions about the connections between the experience of society and the production or reception of literature are no longer being asked. The juxtaposition of literary and extraliterary "series" in late formalism illustrates this problematic, as does the juxtaposition of aesthetic and extraaesthetic experience in reception aesthetics. Whereas formalism and reception aesthetics turn the dissociation of art and life-praxis, radicalized since aestheticism, into the foundation of research, the question of the institutionalization of literature allows, among other things, for the investigation of this dissociation and its social conditions. This is possible because within the concept of institution the production and reception of literature and the experience of society need not be conceived as separate fields.

The (necessary) critique of positivism in literary scholarship eliminates not only problematic research goals (such as "biographism") from the field but also the most important sources of knowledge, on which positivism depends. If the context of the institution concept allows the choice and treatment of artistic material to be reconstituted as the producer's aesthetic and political attitude toward the dominant institution of art or literature, then it implies that the connection between the experience of society and literary production should be investigated through documents, such as essays, letters, and memoirs, which an immanently *literary* scholarship has so far neglected. The same is true for the connection between the experience of society and the reception of literature. Beginning with the supposition that attitudes of reception are not established by great works of art, but rather epochally, that is, institutionalized in class- and group-specific terms, documents of reception should be examined to establish which *general* attitudes of reception are expressed there. The sources are to be interpreted in the context of a historical construction of the functional transformation of literature.[45]

Notes

1. T. W. Adorno, "Thesen zur Kunstsoziologie," in *Seminar: Literatur- und Kunstsoziologie*, Suhrkamp Taschenbuch Wissenschaft, 245 (Frankfurt, 1978), 204.
2. See Adorno, "Wissenschaftliche Erfahrungen in Amerika," *Stichworte: Kritische Modelle 2*, Edition Suhrkamp, 347 (Frankfurt, 1963), 129.
3. Adorno, "Thesen," 206.
4. Peter Bürger, *Theorie der Avantgarde*, Edition Suhrkamp, 727 (Frankfurt, 1973), chaps. 1 and 2; *Theory of the Avant-garde*, trans. Michael Shaw (Minneapolis: University of Minnesota Press, 1984).
5. For an example of the positivistic interpretation of this concept "institution," see N. Fügen, Introduction to *Wege der Literatursoziologie*, ed. N. Fügen (Neuwied, 1971), 19ff, who treats reviews, booksellers, libraries, as well as author and public as "literary institutions." He attempts to understand the "relationship among literary institutions" as a system (24). Apart from some references to the situation in (book) reviewing [*Kritik*], Fügen hardly gets beyond isolated remarks. He cannot establish a systematic comprehension of his object of study because he does not take its historicity into account, as is clear when he takes the essential determination of his argument as the "fictional character of literature"

(21) and thus in a particular, historical conception of literature. For a critique of Fügen's position, see H. Lamprecht, "H. M. Fügen: Die Hauptrichtungen der Literatursoziologie," *Neue Rundschau*, 1966, 530–32, and B. J. Warneken, "Zur Kritik positivistischer Literatursoziologie," in *Literaturwissenschaft und Sozialwissenschaften* (Stuttgart, 1971), 81–150.

6. Thomas Neumann, *Der Künstler in der bürgerlichen Gesellschaft. Entwurf einer Kunstsoziologie am Beispiel der Künsterästhetik Friedrich Schillers*, Soziologische Gegenwartsfragen, 27 (Stuttgart, 1968).

7. If, in the following discussion, an explication of sociological concepts of the institution is dispensed with, it is not because such an explication would break the bounds of this outline but rather because the sociological concepts of the institution are in my opinion barely useful for the historical claims presented here. Nonetheless, we should not dismiss the possibility that, for example, Parsonian theory might offer a descriptive frame for a historically determined type of behavior guided by norms.

8. See Bürger, *Theory of the Avant-garde*, esp. chaps. 1 and 2. See also Kurt Wölfel, "Zur Geschichte des Autonomiebegriffs," in *Historizität in Sprach- und Literaturwissenschaft*, Speeches and Reports at the Stuttgart Germanist Conference 1972, ed. W. Müller-Seidel (Munich, 1974), 563–77; R. Grimminger, "Die ästhetische Versöhnung. Ideologie-kritische Aspekte zum Autonomiebegriff am Beispiel Schillers," in the same volume, 579–97; H. Freier, "Ästhetik und Autonomie. Ein Beitrag zur idealistischen Entfremdungskritik," in *Deutsches Bürgertum und literarische Intelligenz 1750–1800*, ed. B. Lutz, Literaturwissenschaft und Sozialwissenschafter, 3 (Stuttgart, 1973), 329–83; W. Kaiser and G. Mattenklott, "Ästhetik als Geschichtsphilosophie. Die Theorie der Kunst-autonomie in den Schriften Karl Philipp Moritz," in G. Mattenklott and K. Scherpe, eds., *Westberliner Projekt: Grundkurs 18. Jahrhundert*, Literatur im historischen Prozess, 4/1; Scriptor Taschenbücher, 27 (Kronberg, 1974), 243–71.

9. H. Kuhn, "Ästhetik," in *Das Fischer-Lexikon: Literatur* 2:1, ed. W. H. Friedrich and W. Killy (Frankfurt, 1963), 53.

10. In this regard, see Jürgen Habermas's thesis that art in bourgeois society satisfies "residual needs," that is, those needs "that are at the same time illegitimated in the material life-process in bourgeois society": "Bewusstmachende oder rettende Kritik—die Aktualität Walter Benjamins," in *Zur Aktualität Walter Benjamins*, ed. S. Unseld, Suhrkamp Taschenbuch, 150 (Frankfurt, 1972), 192ff.; translated as "Consciousness-raising or Redemptive Criticism: The Contemporaneity of Walter Benjamin," *New German Critique* 17 (Spring 1979): 30–57. We should not equate this social tendency of purposelessness established by the status of autonomy with functionlessness (as I did in *Theory*

of the Avant-garde, 35). As we will see, the concept of autonomy contains a specific functional determination of art.

11. Wölfel, "Zur Geschichtlichkeit des Autonomiebegriffs," 564.

12. In H. Freier's formulation, idealist aesthetics "conceived of the autonomy of art, which is its ideologically suspect product, as a phenomenon of alienation [*Entfremdung*]" ("Ästhetik und Autonomie," 338). This gives us a very broad definition of alienation. If we describe the isolation of art from life-praxis as alienation, it would be difficult to make conceptual sense of the relationship between the institutionalization of art and the critique of alienation.

13. Karl Philipp Moritz, "Das Edelste in der Natur," in *Werke in zwei Bänden*, ed. J. Jahn (Berlin, 1973), 1:236.

14. Friedrich Schiller, "Über die Ästhetische Erziehung des Menschen," in *Sämtliche Werke*, ed. G. Fricke and G. H. Göpfert (Munich, 1967), 5:584, 6th letter.

15. Friedrich Schiller, "Über das Gebrauch des Chors in der Tragödie," in *Sämtliche Werke* 2:816ff.

16. Schiller, "Über die Ästhetische Erziehung," 592, 8th letter.

17. Freier, "Ästhetik und Autonomie," 371.

18. On the concept of ideology, see Peter Bürger, "Ideologiekritik und Literaturwissenschaft," in *Vom Ästhetizismus zum Nouveau Roman*, ed. Peter Bürger (Frankfurt, 1975), 1–22. Also see K. Lenk, *Marx in der Wissensoziologie: Studien zur Rezeption der Marxschen Ideologiekritik*, Soz. Texte, 78 (Neuwied, 1972), chap. 3.

19. See Herbert Marcuse, "Über den affirmativen Charakter der Kultur," *Kultur und Gesellschaft*, Edition Suhrkamp, 101 (Frankfurt, 1968), 56–101; "On the Affirmative Character of Culture," *Negations*, trans. Jeremy Shapiro (Boston: Beacon Press, 1969). In addition to Peter Bürger's work, see Habermas, "Consciousness-raising or Redemptive Criticism," and P. Gorsen, "Transformierte Alltäglichkeit oder Transzendenz der Kunst?" in *Das Unvermögen der Realität* (Berlin, 1974), 129–54.

20. See Claus Offe, *Strukturprobleme des kapitalistischen Staats*, Edition Suhrkamp, 549 (Frankfurt, 1975), 94ff.

21. Paul Valéry, "Berthe Morisot," in *Oeuvres*, ed. J. Hytier, Bibliothèque de la Pleiade (Paris, 1960), 2:1303.

22. On this issue, see Peter Bürger, "Zur Auffassung des Publikums bei Du Bos und Desfontaines," in *Studien zur französischen Frühaufklärung*, Edition Suhrkamp, 525 (Frankfurt, 1972), 44–68, esp., 48ff.

23. Friedrich Schiller, "Über Bürgers Gedichte," in *Sämtliche Werke* 5:970–85, esp. 973ff.

24. See H. J. Frank, *Geschichte des Deutschunterrichts von den Anfängen bis 1945* (Munich, 1973), esp. 296ff., and Christa Bürger, "Zur Dichotomy von

'höherer' und 'volkstümlicher' Bildung," in *Germanistik und Deutschunterricht*, ed. R. Schäfer (Munich, 1979).

25. Hannelore Schlaffer, "Kritik eines Klischees: 'Das Kunstwerk als Ware,'" in *Erweiterung der materialistischen Literaturtheorie durch Bestimmung ihren Grenzen*, ed. Hannelore Schlaffer, Literaturwissenschaft und Sozialwissenschaften, 4 (Stuttgart, 1974), 275.

26. Gerhard Leithaüser, "Kunstwerk und Warenform," in *Seminar: Literatur- und Kunstsoziologie*, 34.

27. In this context, we might recall G. W. F. Hegel's comments, in the preface to the *Phenomenology of Mind*, on the impossibility of formulating a philosophical program, because this formulation must already contain the representation of the subject itself.

28. See R. Mandrou, *La France aux XVIIe et XVIII siècles*, Nouvelle Clio, 33 (Paris, 1967), 134ff.

29. See Norbert Elias, *Das höfische Gesellschaft* (Neuwied, 1969), esp. chap. 5; also F. Nies, *Gattungspoetik und Publikumsstruktur. Zur Geschichte der Sévignébriefe*, Theorie u. Geschichte der Lit. u. der Schönen Künste, 21 (Munich, 1972), 8off.

30. T. W. Adorno, *Versuch über Wagner*, Knaur, 54 (Munich, 1964), 88–89; *In Search of Wagner*, trans. Rodney Livingstone (London, 1981), 83, trans. modified.

31. Jan Mukarovsky, "Aesthetische Funktion, Norm und ästhetische Wert als soziale Fakten," *Kapitel aus der Aesthetik*, Edition Suhrkamp, 428 (Frankfurt, 1970), 36.

32. See Walter Benjamin, "Der Begrif der Kunstkritik in der deutschen Romantik," in *Gesammelte Schriften*, ed. Rolf Tiedemann and H. Schweppenhaüser (Frankfurt, 1974), 1:1:71ff.

33. See G. Mayer's important essay, "Zur Dialektik des musikalischen Materials," *Alternative* 69 (1969): 239–58; also see G. Mayer, *Weltbild—Notenbild. Zur Dialektik des musikalischen Materials*, Röderberg Taschenbuch, 75 (Frankfurt, 1978).

34. T. W. Adorno, *Komposition für den Film*, quoted by Mayer, "Zur Dialektik des musikalischen Materials," 245.

35. T. W. Adorno, "Ideen zur Musiksoziologie," *Klangfiguren: Musikalische Schriften* (Berlin, 1959), 1:27.

36. Hans Robert Jauss, *Literaturgeschichte als Provokation* (Frankfurt, 1970), 173ff.; *Towards an Aesthetics of Reception*, trans. Timothy Bahti (Minneapolis: University of Minnesota Press, 1982), 22ff.

37. Jauss, *Literaturgeschichte*; 172ff.; *Towards an Aesthetics of Reception*, 22ff.

38. On the concept of the intention of the work or text, see Christa Bürger, *Textanalyze als Ideologiekritik* (Frankfurt, 1973), 55.

39. See Peter Bürger, *Die frühen Komödien Pierre Corneilles und das französische Theater um 1630* (Frankfurt, 1971), esp. the afterword, 265 ff.

40. Whereas Corneille's attempted transformation of existing literary material is not met by a corresponding institutionalization of literature, Goethe's *Iphigenia* offers a case of at least delayed correspondence. Goethe's play also stands in an oblique relation to the contemporary institutionalization of literature, both to the late feudal (literature as divertissement) and the bourgeois-Enlightenment (literature as object of bourgeois self-realization) moments. The institution of art presupposed by *Iphigenia* (separation of art from life-praxis) is nonetheless the one that prevails in the course of the further development of bourgeois society. See Christa Bürger, *Der Ursprung der bürgerlichen Institution Kunst im höfischen Weimar. Literatursoziologische Untersuchungen zum klassischen Goethe* (Frankfurt, 1977), and "Classical Processes of Dissociation: Goethe's *Iphigenia*" in this volume. Christa Bürger's study tests the conceptual tools developed here on a concrete object of study, analyzing the sociohistorical conditions of the transformation of the institution of literature.

41. See the case study by Peter Bürger, "Zum Funktionswandel der Literatur in der Epoche des entstehenden Absolutismus: La Querelle du Cid," in *Bildung und Ausbildung*, ed. R. Kloepfer (Munich, 1979); translated in this volume as "The Functional Transformation of Dramatic Literature in the Era of Emergent Absolutism."

42. See Jochen Schulte-Sasse, *Literarische Wertung*, Sammlung Metzler, 98 (Stuttgart, 1976), chap. 1.

43. See *Zur Dichotomie von höhere und niedere Literatur*, Hefte für kritische Literaturwissenschaft, 3 (Frankfurt, 1980).

44. Theodor Adorno to Walter Benjamin, 18 March 1936, in T. W. Adorno, *Über Walter Benjamin*, ed. Rolf Tiedemann, Bibliothek Suhrkamp, 260 (Frankfurt, 1970), 129.

45. See Jacques Dubois, *L'Institution de la littérature* (Brussels, 1978). Following the work of Pierre Bourdieu, among others, Dubois comes to conclusions similar in some respects to those reached here; see esp. his chaps. 1 and 2.

2.

The Functional Transformation of Dramatic Literature in the Era of Emergent Absolutism

Preliminary Remark:
The Problem of Literary Evolution

Traditional interpretation of single works attempts to grasp the meaning of a work, which is in turn conceived of either as something preexistent in the work subject to the recipient's interpretation or as something to be originally produced by him or her. In the first case, the stable point is the objectivity of the work; in the second, it is the subjectivity of the interpreter. Traditional hermeneutics resolves this dilemma by blurring the opposition (Gadamer speaks of the fusion of horizons [*Horizontver-schmelzung*]).[1] The methodological limitations of this approach lie above all in the fact that the work of the past and its present-day appropriation cannot be clearly distinguished. For example, Serge Doubrovsky interprets *l'heroisme corneillien* as existentialist self-assertion. He thus updates Corneille by making the playwright his contemporary. In order to do this, he has to erase the historical distance which separates him from his subject. The danger of this kind of updating is obvious. Simply put, in this interpretation, Corneille's specifically feudal self-assertion becomes self-assertion as such. This radical presentism not only distorts the work of the past—any interpretation does that up to a point; it also risks importing

This essay is part of a research project—Literatur als Institution: Zum historischen Wandel der gesellschaftlichen Funktion der Literatur—undertaken with Gerhart Leithäuser and supported by the University of Bremen. See also *Aufklärung und bürgerliche Öffentlichkeit*, ed. Christa Bürger, Peter Bürger, and Jochen Schulte-Sasse (Frankfurt, 1980).

traditional elements (such as feudal modes of conduct) unexamined into the present.

Historicism claims to be an alternative to presentist interpretation. But the historicist who wants to become a contemporary of the past work also blurs the distinction between past and present, only in the opposite direction. Whereas the presentist interpreter imports unexamined elements of the past into the present, the historicist runs the risk of subordinating present-day aesthetic norms and political opinions to those of the past. Interpreters may remain unaware of this blurring because it usually occurs at the moment at which the problem is posed and with the very choice of analytic categories. Moreover, the historicist shares with the presentist the notion that the work is accessible "as such" and thus abstracts the work from the process of tradition that makes the work a work, namely, an object worthy of interpretive attention.[2]

In order to avoid this false opposition between historicism and radical presentism, we must try to break the illusion of the immediate accessibility of the work. That can happen most effectively if we make the presuppositions about both (past) emergence and (present-day) appropriation the object of analysis. This is possible if we pose the question of the historical transformation of literature's social function. The work, which owes its emergence to a particular institutionalization of literature, is appropriated by modern interpreters in the context of a different institutionalization. Instead of blurring the contradiction between past work and present-day appropriation in the manner of the fusion of horizons, the sociological-institutional approach tries to make that contradiction visible. In this way the hermeneutic link to the present is not breached (for the question of the functional transformation of literature comes to light owing to the crisis of the institution of literature at the present time) but may at least be clarified.[3]

The question of the historical transformation of the social function of literature relates to the problem of literary evolution. The solution proposed by Russian formalism is well known, not least because of its reformulation by reception aesthetics. According to this approach, literary evolution can be understood as a process of "automatization" of artistic means or principles of construction. Repeated use of the same artistic means of production results in the loss of their effectiveness (automatization), which compels authors to apply new (or old and forgotten) means.[4] In reception-aesthetic terms: the new work explodes the horizon of expectations of the public. Useful as the Russian Formalist attempts to formulate the problem of literary evolution are, their proposed solution is problematic, because it depends on a superhistorical generalization. The ongoing renewal of artistic means is a relatively late phenomenon which must be seen in conjunction with the emergence of the modern; it cannot therefore count as a general principle of literary evolution.[5] Corneille's *Cid* does not explode the contemporary audience's horizons of expectations but, rather, fulfills them in an ideal way. The same is true of Racine's plays. The evolution theory of the Russian Formalists, formulated as it is on the basis of the literature of aestheticism and the avant-garde movements, evidently does not apply to the literature of feudal absolutist society. We must therefore try to formulate a more complex theory of evolution which will break with the principle of immanent development.[6]

We must first establish that literary evolution cannot be understood as a series of single works but rather as a development shaped by the limit conditions of literary production and reception, which we may call the institution of literature. This concept refers to those dominant conceptions of literature (functional determinants) prevailing in a society (or in individual classes or ranks).[7] Literary evolution should therefore be primarily investigated in the context of the evolution of the institutionalized functional determinants of literature. The question is, which social forces promote which conceptions of literature and with what means? The *Querelle du Cid* will be examined in the light of this question. The debate is interesting because it is one of the most significant disputes over the institutionalization of literature. For the *doctrine classique* at issue here does not merely hold sway over feudal absolutist society; it has also been adopted—albeit in modified form—in bourgeois society. The persistence of the classical rule-bound aesthetic [*Regelästhetik*] is significant not merely for historical reasons but for what it represses: the aesthetic of "tragicomedy" to which *Le Cid* subscribes. At issue is the question whether the rule-bound aesthetic prevailing beyond absolutism also represses moments of immediacy and spontaneity which are still expressed in *Le Cid* but banished from the later classical tragedy.

It would surely be wrong, however, to examine literary evolution solely on the level of institutionalized conceptions of literature and their transformation. Even within a given institutionalization there are obviously significant processes of transformation. These can best be grasped in the domain of the *artistic material*. The concept should not refer to something "extra-artistic" but rather to the state of evolution of literary forms carrying a certain content in a given period. It is certainly legitimate to interpret *Le Cid* as a complete articulation of tragicomic material; we can nonetheless note distinctions in the treatment of this material. If these distinctions are sufficiently noteworthy, they may provide the foundation for an attempt to grasp the value [*Gehalt*] of the play.

La Querelle du Cid: The Institutionalization of the *Doctrine Classique*

Traditional literary historiography has, to be sure, noted the *querelle du Cid* as a historical fact but has not acknowledged its significance as a source for a historicosociological understanding of literature's functional transformation in the era of emergent absolutism. We may cite Gustave Lanson as a particularly crass example of a faulty evaluation: "The dispute over *Le Cid* shows us only the exasperation of jealous and impotent rivals. There is no principle or artistic doctrine at stake here."[8] This refusal even to take cognizance of the object of debate can be satisfactorily explained only with an investigation of the function of traditional literary historiography in the context of a critique of the institution of art/literature in bourgeois society. Traditional literary historiography in France well into the twentieth century could not make sense of the *querelle du Cid*. On the one hand, the superhistorical validity of the *doctrine classique* was beyond doubt; on the other, however, *Le Cid*, which was criticized in the *querelle* in the name of this doctrine, was treated as the first classical tragedy: "*Le Cid*'s value lay in firmly establishing the notion of classical tragedy and, for this reason, it is a significant date in the history of art."[9] If one canonizes as classical tragedy a play which fully developed the affective means of tragicomedy around 1630 and which Corneille himself identified as "tragicomedy" in the first edition, it becomes impossible to conceive of the *querelle* as a struggle between the (old) tragicomic aesthetic and the (new) rule-bound classical aesthetic.

Even Antoine Adam, who is responsible for, among other things, challenging the primacy of classicism in his *Histoire de la littérature française au XVIIe siècle*, does not offer a sociohistorical analysis of the aesthetic positions articulated in the debate. He focuses his attention rather on the question of a possible change in Cardinal Richelieu's taste for the play and bases this surmise on intrigues (without documentary evidence).[10] What seems to me more important than this question is the fact, demonstrated by Jean Chapelain's letters, that Richelieu was concerned not about the judgment of *Le Cid* by the Academy, whose cultural political significance he wished to extend, but rather about a condemnation of the play. In these letters, Chapelain, who had outlined the *Sentiments de l'Académie Française sur la tragi-comédie du Cid* (Thoughts of the French Academy on the tragicomedy *Le Cid*), attempts, in distinctly wounded tones, to make clear to Richelieu that he had refuted Scudéry's critique on a number of (unimportant) points, since advocates for *Le Cid* would otherwise see the Academy as partisan. Nonetheless, he stresses his willingness to respect the cardinal's wishes on any modifications.[11] In a later letter to Guez de Balzac, Chapelain speaks explicitly of the "persecution of *Le Cid*": "The thought of the persecution of *Le Cid* is still with me after five months." [12] There can be no doubt as to the fact that Richelieu managed to push through his absolutist cultural program against the most successful play of the time. At issue is whether the content of the play also stands in the way of the aspirations of absolutism.

Before we examine two central documents of the *querelle* in light of the functional transformation of dramatic literature in the context of emergent absolutism, it may be useful to recall briefly the material conditions governing the French theater in the first quarter of the seventeenth century.[13] The material conditions of theater production should also be seen in relation to prevailing general conceptions of theater. Before 1629 there were no stationary theaters in Paris but only traveling troupes. Playwrights were generally attached to a particular troupe, for whom they worked for a fixed fee. The plays, intended exclusively for performance, were rarely published. Alexander Hardy, for example, is said to have written over six hundred plays, of which only forty were published, and then only long after their performance. If we remember the social disdain for the actor's trade, it becomes clear that playwrights could hardly develop anything like artistic self-consciousness, since their plays were above all intended to satisfy the entertainment needs of an extremely diffuse public.

At the end of the 1620s, significant changes occured: in Paris, two stationary theaters were founded and a number of young writers, among them Corneille and Rotrou, began to write for the theater. Most of the plays were published and sometimes reprinted several times.[14] This suggests a change in habits of reception. Plays were now no longer only viewed in the theater; they were also read. The playwrights, in turn, developed a certain artistic self-consciousness, albeit limited by dependence on patrons. These changes should be understood in the context of an emerging salon culture developed by the politically disempowered nobility. These changes are relevant to the presuppositions of the *querelle*. The fact that this sort of battle could erupt and that the public could take part presupposes an inordinate interest in the theater. The fact that it affected Richelieu himself demonstrates that literature had become a politically relevant issue.

In the secondary literature, the *querelle* is treated again and again as the expression of envious rival playwrights, who wanted to contest Corneille's extraordinary success with the audience. This kind of psychologizing interpretation seems to me to misunderstand the historically specific articulation of this rivalry. At issue in the *querelle* was evidently not merely *Le Cid* but also an occasional poem, "Excuse à Aristide," in which Corneille reveals an artistic self-confidence that was unheard of for his time:

Mon travail sans appuy monte sur le Théâtre,
Chacun en liberté l'y blasme ou l'idolatre . . .
Je satisfaits ensemble et people et courtisans
Et mes vers en tous lieux sont mes seuls partisans
Par leur seule beauté ma plume est estimée
Je ne dois qu'à moy seul toute ma Rénommée

[My work mounts the boards without support. / Anyone is free to despise or adore it. / I satisfy both the people and the court, / and my verses are everywhere my only patrons. / By their beauty alone my pen is judged. / I owe my fame to myself alone].[15]

These lines are significant in at least two senses: (1) Corneille bases his self-confidence exclusively on the artistic products of his labor, whereas Georges de Scudéry, whose self-praise is no less ardent than his subsequent opponent in the *querelle*, grounds his authority on his noble origins. This position corresponds to Scudéry's conception of art as "amusement" [*divertissement*]: "La Poesie me tient lieu de divertissement agreable, & non pas d'occupation sérieuse [Poetry is for me a pleasant distraction and not a serious occupation]."[16] Whereas Corneille complains in the "Excuse à Aristide" that the producer does not profit from his verses ("et les vers à présent / Aux meilleurs du mestier n'apportent que du vent [And at present verses bring nothing but the wind to the best of the craft]" Gasté, 64), Scudéry had explicitly emphasized, in the foreword to his *Ligdamon et Lidias* that he received no money from either the printer or the actors for his play: "The printer and the actors will confirm that I did not sell them what they could not buy from me." (2) Corneille recognizes the audience seeing the performance alone as the agent validating dramatic work and thus implicitly rejects the authority of learned criticism as well as the judgment of patrons. That this self-confident attitude adopted by Corneille was unusual for the period can be seen in Chapelain's correspondence, in which he thanks Richelieu for the latter's corrections of *La Pucelle* in the most subservient way.[17] That Richelieu's dislike of the sense of independence displayed by Corneille could have practical consequences for the latter can be seen in the case of Balzac, who earned the disfavor of the cardinal by, among other things, neglecting to dedicate his work to him.[18]

It is not easy to establish whether Corneille's untypical sense of independence ought to be seen as an old feudal sense of freedom rebelling against absolutist centralism, or whether it already constitutes the self-assertion of the bourgeois author. The fact that Corneille conceived of the activity of writing as labor, for which he expected (adequate) compensation, and that he conceived of the audience as the public in its entirety ("the people and the court") as the agent of literary judgment, encourages us to interpret his position as bourgeois. This does not imply that Corneille expressed the interests of the contemporary bourgeoisie in his plays such as *Le Cid* (which is certainly not the case), but only that he brings to light, in "Excuse à Aristide," a mode of conduct that challenges those material conditions of literary production that are still determined by dependence on a patron. Further evidence for this interpretation can be found in Corneille's dismissal of Scudéry's pride in his nobility as irrelevant to the dispute. As he writes in the *Lettre apologétique*: "We do not need to know that you are noble or braver than me in order to judge how much better *Le Cid* is than *L'Amant libéral*" (Gasté, 147). In contrast, Scudéry had articulated his understanding of himself as an aristocrat by representing his critique as a chivalric battle:

J'ataque le Cid non pas son Autheur; j'en veux à son Ouvrage et non point à sa personne; Et comme les combats et la civilité ne sont pas incompatibles, je veux baiser le floret, dont je prétends luy porter une botte franche.

[I am attacking *Le Cid*, not its author; I have in mind his work and not at all his person. And, since battles and chivalry are not at all incompatible, I would like to possess the flower whose fresh bouquet I intend to give him.] (Gasté, 72)

Thus far, we have limited the discussion to replacing the psychologizing interpretation of the dispute around *Le Cid* with a sociological interpretation of the self-image of the chief protagonists. This has brought us to the object of the *querelle*. At issue is not merely the problem of rules but also the contest between two distinct institutionalizations of dramatic literature. These can be differentiated in terms of their respective functional determination, attitude of reception, and in their artistic material; each in turn presupposes different material conditions of literature distribution.

Scudéry's *Observations sur "Le Cid"* opens with the distinction between true beauties [*beautés effectives*] and illusory beauties [*beautés d'illusion*]. The problem concealed behind this distinction is one that Scudéry had already articulated in previous years in the forewords and dedications of his own plays. The theatrical image can deceive even the literati; only in quiet, private study can one judge the literary value of a dramatic work:

Ie sçay que l'esclat du Theatre en donne aux vers, & que l'oreille la plus iuste peut estre deceue par vne mauvaise chose ditte de bône grace; mais il n'en sera pas ainsi dans vn Cabinet où le silence, la solitude, & le loisir vous permettront d'examiner plus exactement ce CRIMINEL.

[I know that theater shines in poetry and that even the best ear can be deceived by a bad thing called good taste, but it is not the case in a private room in which silence, solitude, and leisure allow you to examine this CRIMINAL more carefully.] [19]

Scudéry uses the same argumentation at the outset of his *Observations*:

Aussi ne m'estonnay-je pas beaucoup que le Peuple qui porte le jugement dans les yeux, se laisse tromper par celuy de tous les sens, le plus facile à decevoir: Mais que cette vapeur grossiere, qui se forme dans le Parterre ait pu s'eslever jusqu'aux Galleries, et qu'un fantosme ait abusé le sçavoir comme l'ignorance, et la Cour aussi bien que le Bourgeois, j'avoüe que ce prodige m'estonne, et que ce n'est qu'un bizarre evenement que je trouve LE CID merveilleux.

[In addition, I am not very surprised that the People, who judge with their eyes, allow themselves to be fooled by the sense of sight which, of all the senses, is the easiest to deceive. But I am astonished that this coarse vapor rising from the pit has managed to reach the galleries and that a phantom has manipulated the knowledge as well as the ignorance of both court and bourgeoisie. I confess that this phenomenon astonishes me and that, in the midst of this bizarre event I found LE CID extraordinary.] (Gasté, 71)

Scudéry juxtaposes two different attitudes toward dramatic literature, which he attributes to particular audiences and evaluates accordingly. Judgment on the basis of immediate sensation at the performance is characteristic of the ignoble sector of the audience (*peuple* or *bourgeois*), which is also seen as uneducated (*l'ignorance*). On the other hand, Scudéry attributes to the courtly nobility ("La Cour") the ability to judge the play according to rational criteria (*le sçavoir*). The difficulty facing Scudéry is the fact that *Le Cid* received undivided praise from all sectors of the audience. He has therefore to prove that the educated members of the audience ("La Cour") allowed themselves to be deceived by the impression of the performance.[20] Turning to the rules of Renaissance poetics, Scudéry hopes to dissociate the aesthetic judgment of dramatic works from the theatrical illusion which depends on sensuous deception and establish that judgment on rational foundations.[21] At the same time, he foregrounds the division of the audience into educated and uneducated, so that the lines between ranks become the dividing line in modes of receptions as well.

To be sure, we cannot treat Scudéry's presentation as a representation of the actual audience. That audience—as the unalloyed success of *Le Cid* demonstrates—is precisely not divided into different factions; instead the unity of the audience transcends rank. Scudéry, on the other hand, outlines a cultural program. He attacks the prevailing institutionalization of dramatic literature in that he attempts to secure the place of the aristocracy as the primary culture-bearing social rank. (At this point, in the 1630s, the distinction between court and feudal nobility is not yet as developed as it would become during the Fronde.)

The appeal to Horatian formulas, according to which entertaining instruction is the goal of poetry ("Dramatic poetry was invented to instruct in delighting" [Gasté, 79]), should be understood as an attempt to discipline an entertainment theater directed exclusively toward the immediate cultivation of the audience's pleasure. To be sure, the pleasure that was offered to the audiences of the comedy and tragicomedy of the 1630s was already purified of so-called crude comic effects (fights, sexual innuendo, etc.) and limited to achieving a convincing illusion of dramatic situations; these in turn could be enjoyed insofar as they were judged in purely artistic rather than moral terms.[22] At first glance, the reference to the instructive function of the theater appears to contradict the courtly aristocratic cultural program with its focus on divertissement; we should nonetheless be aware of the significance of instruction in this context. In these plays, instruction should be seen in the light of the inculcation of sociocultural norms defined by rank, which should strike the audience or audience elite as "good morals" [bonnes moeurs] or "verisimilitude" [vraisemblance]. Scudéry takes the Aristotelian rule of verisimilitude to mean a demand for the correspondence between the mode of conduct of the characters and the moral and social norms of an elite rank. That becomes clear when he criticizes Corneille's characters for their deficient correspondence to the prevailing notions of conduct appropriate to rank. So Scudéry censures Don Sancho's conduct as unworthy of an "homme de coeur," when Sancho, after losing the duel to Rodrigue, takes up the humiliating task of conveying the victor's dagger to Chimène, dismissing this moment as a theatrical effect ("procédure trop romanesque" [Gasté, 83]). Likewise he criticizes Doña Uraques's love for Rodrigue, her social inferior, as unworthy of the infanta (Gasté, 82), and the unkingly conduct of Don Fernand for staging a performance in order to discover Chimène's true feelings ("He ought to treat the person of the king with more respect, since we are taught that he is sacred, and to act as if the king were on the throne of Castille and not on the stage at Mondory" [Gasté, 93]). The performance set up by Don Fernand is treated like a theatrical effect and rejected in the name of an absolute conception of the gravity and the untouchable character of the king.

We should nonetheless emphasize that some of the arguments that

Scudéry directs against *Le Cid* appear to contradict the interpretation proposed here: in particular, his critique of the inhumanity of the honor code that compels Chimène to recognize as legitimate the mode of conduct of Rodrigue, the man who kills her father: "You have done no more than the duty of a noble man" [*homme du bien*]. When Scudéry accuses Corneille of unnatural feelings ("he casts aside natural feelings and moral precepts" [Gasté, 83]), he seems to be arguing in the name of a concept of universal humanity which contradicts the conception of social hierarchy outlined above. It would certainly be wrong to wrest conceptual coherence from the *Observations* at all costs, but we ought nonetheless to attempt an understanding of the contradictions. That understanding should be possible if we realize that absolutism bore a contradictory relation to the old feudal nobility. Putting it very schematically, absolutism secured the survival of the feudal nobility by rendering its members politically impotent. When Scudéry upholds the principles of a hierarchical society and criticizes Corneille's characters for behavior inappropriate to their rank on the one hand, while, on the other hand, arguing against an outdated code of honor in terms that resemble a bourgeois moral conception, both moments of his critique are compatible with Richelieu's politics, in particular, with his attempt to break the outmoded independence of the feudal nobility without casting doubt on the principle of a hierarchical society.

A further contradiction in Scudéry's argument also deserves mention, since he acknowledges that the rule-bound aesthetic which he represents has in no way gained the status of an unquestioned foundation for aesthetic evaluation. When Scudéry dismisses the infanta and Don Sancho as superfluous characters ("Both have so little to do with the body of the play and are hardly necessary to the performance" [Gasté, 83]), he invokes the principle of unity of action and objects to its violation.[23] At the same time, on the first page of his text, he maintains that, as a "tragicomedy," *Le Cid* is not subject to the unity of action but, rather, to an aesthetic of "diversité" (Gasté, 74). He criticizes the play because it has no plot that might keep the spectators in suspense, only to release the tension by surprising them at the end: "There is no diversity, no plot, no knot" [*Noeu*] (Gasté, 74).

The contradiction is significant for several reasons. It makes clear that the representative of a rule-bound aesthetic who wants to ground aesthetic evaluation on the foundation of rational criteria legitimated by the tradition is still held hostage by another aesthetic. This aesthetic encourages the audience's involvement with events on stage, an involvement achieved by effects of suspense and surprise, as the decisive measure of the value of dramatic works. In other words, the developing institutionalization of dramatic literature, which we may characterize as that of the absolutist court, was not yet fully established by the end of the 1630s even in the work of its champions. The fact that Scudéry uses the conceptual apparatus of the very tragicomedy that he is attacking demonstrates that the institutionalization of the rule-bound aesthetic installs a cultural program against the prevailing habits of aesthetic perception and judgment of the producers and recipients of dramatic works. Whereas Scudéry willingly takes on the role of instrument in this cultural program, Chapelain does so not without (inner) resistance.

The above-mentioned passage is significant for a third reason. It shows that the different institutionalizations of dramatic literature also correspond to distinctions in the generic framework [*Gattungsgefüge*]. The preabsolutist divertissement theater that relies on the unity of the audience across diverse social classes is most fully expressed in the tragicomedy. In contrast, the rule-bound aesthetic is focused primarily on tragedy. How the framework of dramatic genres undergo essential changes as the new institutionalization of dramatic literature establishes itself cannot be gone into here. We should note nonetheless that the majority of plays in the preabsolutist theater tended, as their generic classifications suggest (*tragi-comédie, pastorale, comédie*), in the general direction of tragicomedy. This was also partly true of tragedy. The use of certain affective means largely independent of particular genres took precedence over genre-specific choices. Nonetheless, notions of a generic hierarchy were proposed. With the institutionalization of rules, the framework of dramatic genres was hierarchically ordered; because of the social rank of its characters, tragedy occupied the highest point. At the same time, those genres not legitimated by the Aristotelian tradition fell into disrepute. These changes also affected book production. After 1640, hardly any pastorals were published; tragicomedy, the most successful genre of the 1630s, evinced a distinct retreat, while the production of tragedies experienced an extraordinary increase (over eighty published tragedies in the 1640s as against thirty in the previous decade).[24] Even if tragicomedy slid into insignificance only in the 1660s, the staying power of the absolutist court's cultural program should not be written off.

One particular document in the defense of *Le Cid* deserves center stage:

the anonymous *Jugement du Cid, composé par un bourgeois de Paris, marguiller de sa paroisse* (Gasté, 230–40). Just as, at the beginning of his essay, Scudéry articulates an understanding of himself as aristocrat and also speaks dismissively of "le bourgeois" and "le peuple," the anonymous author of the *Jugement* notes his social status at the outset in the subtitle of his text. He takes on the role of speaking for that sector of the audience which produced the success of *Le Cid*, but which had not yet been represented in the *querelle*. He would like his contribution to be understood as "the feeling of honest common people [*honnestes gens d'entre le peuple*]" (Gasté, 231). He explicitly attacks another of Corneille's partisans, whom he accuses of defending courtly morality and a pedantic rationality: "The pedant who has taken up his cause seems to take more care to defend his display of court morality and to appear as a great logician than to do anything to Corneille's advantage" (Gasté, 231). This testimony not only clearly defends the anticourt position of the *bourgeois de Paris;* it also confirms my interpretation of Scudéry by establishing the connection between the debate on rational rules and court morality. In accordance with his programmatic rejection of a learned debate on *Le Cid*, the *bourgeois de Paris* limits his argument in the first instance to recalling his experiences as a spectator:

> Je n'ay jamais leu Aristote, et ne sçay point les regles du theatre, mais je regle le merite des pieces selon le *plaisir* qu j'y reçoy. Celle-cy a je ne sçay quoi de charmant dans son accident extraordinaire; et il n'y a personne qui apres avour veu le mariage resolu de deux Amans, *n'entre en de grandes craintes* pour eux aussi tost que les peres commencent à se quereller. Qui ne soit *esmeu* voyant l'affront que reçoit Dom Diegue: Qui ne soit *troublé* voyant le commandement qu'il fait à son fils de le venger; et qui ne *s'attendrisse* de pitié voyant le combat en Rodrigue entre son honneur et son amour. Mais jamais rien n'a plus *transporter* les spectateurs qu'alors que Rodrigue ayant tué le Comte, vient chez Chimène luy demander la mort, et met le mesme combat en son esprit entre son amour et son honneur.

[I have never read Aristotle and know nothing about the rules of theater, but I rule on the merit of plays according to the *pleasure* they give me. This play has something inexplicably charming in its extraordinary arbitrariness. There is nobody who, after seeing the resolute marriage of the two lovers, is *not taken with great fear* once the two fathers begin to fight. Who is not *moved* on seeing the affront which Dom Diegue receives; who is not *troubled* on seeing him command his son to avenge him, and who is not *softened* by pity on seeing Rodrigue torn between his honor and his love. But nothing has ever transported the spectators as much as when Rodrigue, having killed the count, comes to Chimène to demand her death and sets in motion the same conflict in his soul between love and honor.] (Gasté, 231)

Here the judgment of dramatic works on the basis of pleasure displaces judgment on the basis of rules. This pleasure lies in identifying with the protagonist of the play. Verbs which express the spectator's emotional involvement with the events on stage dominate the text.

The beginning of the *Jugement* gives us the impression that the author has succeeded in building up a consistent counterposition to Scudéry's: he emphasizes the priority of the performance as against the printed text, and also the priority of pleasurable emotional involvement of the spectator in the events on stage as against the learned criticism oriented toward concepts such as verisimilitude and decorum [*bienséance*], theater for entertainment of a broad public including the "people" instead of rule-bound court theater. The consistency with which the *bourgeois de Paris* presents this position is evident in his disapproval of the play's publication. Plays like *Le Cid*, so he argues, are intended for public performance; in printing the play, Corneille himself had given rise to the presupposition that his text could be judged according to the standards of aesthetic criticism, which it withstands as badly as other plays of the period.

Ces sortes de pieces qui se recitent dans les lieux publics, ne veulent pas estre considerées de si pres: elles n'ont besoin que d'un certain esclat, et il ne nous importe qu'il soit trompeur pourvu qu'il plaise: comme ce seroit folie dans les habits de ballets d'employer de l'or fin, puisque le faux y paroist tout autant. C'est la raison pour laquelle Corneille ne devoit point faire imprimer Le Cid: il devoit se contenter d'avoir estré si applaudy, sans souffrir que l'on l'examinast.

[The kinds of plays that are presented in public places are not intended to be scrutinized so closely; they need only a certain sparkle, and we should not be concerned if they deceive so long as they please, just as it would be foolish to use fine gold in ballet costumes when false will do as well. This is the reason that Corneille should not have published *Le Cid*: he ought to be content to have been so enthusiastically applauded, without undergoing scrutiny.] (Gasté, 232)

The author's position is clear, first, in his argument in terms of a "people's theater" [*Volkstheater*] whose goal is to satisfy the desire for entertainment of its audience and, second, in his acknowledgment, however reluctantly, of the standards of a rule-bound poetics. The author's admission that plays like *Le Cid* emit a deceptive sparkle (*eclat trompeur*) recalls Scudéry's distinction between illusory and true beauties. In contrast to Scudéry, the author of *Jugement* nonetheless believes that plays are intended for performance, that is, for the creation of a momentary illusion: this priority makes the type of perfection demanded by critics in favor of rules superfluous.

Moreover, his judgment of *Le Cid* remains correspondingly ambivalent. He acknowledges the validity of Scudéry's critique, whose arguments he takes on point by point. He opposes to this critique the point that the play was well received by the "peuple" despite or even because of its evident faults.

Je sçay qu'il n'y a point d'apparence qu'une fille ait voulu espouser le meurtrier de son pere, mais cela a donné subjet de dire de belles pointes. Je sçay bien que Dom Gormas est un fanfaron, mais ce qu'il dit n'est pas desagreable au peuple. . . . Je sçay que le Roy devoit avoir donné ordre au port, ayant esté adverty du dessin des Mores; mais s'il eust fait, le Cid ne luy eust pas rendu ce grand service qui l'oblige à luy pardonner. Je sçay bien que l'Infante est un personnage inutile, mais il falloit remplir la piece. Je sçay bien que Dom Sanche est un pauvre badin, mais il falloit qu'il apportast son espée, afin de faire peur à Chimène. . . . Je sçay bien la Scene est le Palais, tantost la place publique, tantost la chambre de Chimène, tantost l'appartement de l'Infante, tantoste du Roy, et tout cela si confus que l'on se trouve quelquefois de l'un dans l'autre par miracle, sans avoir passé aucune porte: mais l'Auteur avoit besoin de tout cela.

[I know that there appears to be nothing more at issue than a girl willing to marry the man who murdered her father, but this becomes the subject of much wit. I know that Don Gormas is a braggart, but what he says is not disagreeable to the people. . . . I know that the king, having been warned of Mores's plan, should have given orders to the port, but if he had done so, the Cid would not have done him the great service which obliged the king to pardon him. I know that the infanta is a superfluous character, but the play must be complete. I know that Don Sancho is a poor joker, but he must have his sword so as to frighten Chimène. . . . I know that the scene is the palace, whether the infanta's apartment or the king's and that all the coming and going between locations without going through any doors, as if by miracle, is very confusing, but the author needed all this.] (Gasté, 233f.)

The argument has the same structure throughout: the acknowledgment of the fault is either juxtaposed with the brute fact that Corneille apparently could not avoid it, or with the insight that this very fault made possible a particular effect on the audience. Thus the implausible action (Chimène marries her father's murderer) or character (Don Gormas as a braggart) please the audience precisely because they allow the formulation of particular points. The inconsistency in the king's behavior is necessary to emphasize the uniqueness of Rodrigue's military achievement. Don Sancho, defeated by Rodrigue in the duel, has to bring Chimène Rodrigue's dagger so that she (and the audience) will mistakenly believe that Rodrigue has been killed by Sancho. The author of the *Jugement* goes so far as to cast doubt as to whether Corneille's characters act at all in a reasonable manner ("to tell the truth, all the characters appear to be mad" [Gasté, 237]). Nonetheless, unlike Scudéry, he does not claim that this madness violates morality but, rather, emphasizes the contradiction between word and deed. The evaluative criterion here is thus not a moral norm but the question whether the characters act rationally in the light of their goals. When Rodrigue stays in Don Gormas's house after killing him in the duel, his behavior is not morally reprehensible but extremely careless, since Gormas's servants could kill him. Chimène, too, does not behave in a manner that matches the dramatic situation, when, instead of arousing the interest of the king, she offers witticisms: "Instead of attempting to move the king, she offers witticisms and the king has to tell her: 'My dear, your wit is charming but you are not suffering'" (Gasté, 236).

The position of the *bourgeois de Paris* is the following: precisely those moments in the play that Scudéry rightly criticizes as implausible are responsible for the success of the performance: "to be sure, the subject is appealing only because of its bizarreness and extravagance" (Gasté, 235). The *Jugement* offers another insight into the reception attitude still prevailing in Corneille's time, namely, that of that sector of the audience designated *peuple*. The object of attention and pleasure is not so much the degree to which characters' conduct is appropriate to their roles or situations, nor the coherence of the plot, and certainly not the play as a whole, but rather *individual affective elements* [*einzelne Wirkungselemente*]. These include virtuoso rhetorical wit [*pointes*] as well as situations that permit an intense emotional involvement. In contrast, the demand for unity of action and the principle of character coherence associated with the rule of decorum entail the notion of the self-containment of the literary work whose parts necessarily depend on the whole.

Let us now attempt to summarize a few results. I have treated *la querelle du Cid* not as the object of an investigation into the contemporary reception of a successful play but, rather, as a way of revealing in the debate the historical transformation of the social function of dramatic literature in its social determination. This transformation affects the various levels of the institutionalization of dramatic literature, aesthetic norms, institutionalized reception attitudes, and artistic material (the changes in the generic framework).

Preabsolutist theater can be characterized as a theater of divertissement, which satisfies the entertainment needs of an audience that transcends rank. The experience of pleasurable identification with the events on stage and the admiration of rhetorical virtuosity constitute pleasure in the theater and function also as the criterion of aesthetic validation. Insofar as the theater experience as a whole, rather than the printed text, is the object of this aesthetic validation deemed interchangeable with pleasurable experience, we can say that aesthetic norms are not yet autonomous. The audience's entertainment needs are adequately realized in the genre of tragicomedy, whose structural characteristics are common to many plays, including those not specifically called tragicomedies: a profusion of events, sudden interruptions of the action, concentration on the motif of feigning [*feinte*]. These and other characteristics of tragicomedy which are central to the generic framework of drama in the period ensure the audience's emotional involvement in the events on stage.

The institutionalization of the *doctrine classique* is a process that presupposes certain changes in the material conditions and social recognition of theater: construction of stationary theaters, the improved social condition of playwrights, increase in the number of published plays. These changes should not, however, be seen as the cause of the process. To be sure, the sudden increase in the number of published plays may lead to the conclusion that at least part of the theater audience also read and so abandoned the hitherto institutionalized reception that had maintained the priority of the theater experience. The changes in the attitude of reception mentioned here are doubtless necessary for the successful dissemination of the *doctrine classique;* yet the rules cannot be derived from these changes. Likewise, the institutionalization of the *doctrine classique* can hardly be attributed to the arrival of a great literary work which, in the terms of formalist evolution theory, replaces automatized procedures with new ones or explodes a given horizon of expectation. On the contrary, *Le Cid*, which provided the spark to ignite the dispute, completely fulfilled the audience's expectations with its adept employment of the tragicomic effects. The significant functional transformation of literature (whose effects went beyond aristocratic society), which resulted in the institutionalization of the *doctrine classique,* is the result of a courtly aristocratic cultural program.

In a letter to Boisrobert, one of Richelieu's deputies, dated 24 January 1635 (before the *querelle du Cid*), Chapelain writes:

> Je n'ay pas, dis-je, voulu qu'on ait peu de dire avec raison que Monseigneur [Richelieu] remettant tous les arts en honneur, et en laissant à la posterité tant de monuments publics, dans lesquels il entre en une si grande émulation avec les plus grands hommes de l'Antiquité, la seule poésie, laquelle il honore de sa protection particulière, demeurast sous luy dans la bassesse et le desreglement, et qu'en cela il cédast au moins à ces grands personnages qui l'ont fait fleurir et lesquels il esgalle ou surpasse mesme en toutes autres choses.

> [I did not want to imply of my lord (Richelieu), restoring honor to all the arts and leaving to posterity so many public monuments through which he emulates the greatest men of the ancient world, that poetry alone, which he honors with special protection, has remained under his tutelage in a state of lowliness and disorder, or that, in this, he cedes to those great men who made poetry flourish, whom he equals or even surpasses in all other things.] [25]

Here, rules are understood as the necessary condition for the emergence of great poetry which in its turn is seen as a necessary component of great power. As suitable means for developing a significant vernacular literature which might be compared to antiquity, the rules of the classical doctrine of art, which appear to establish only formal criteria for the perfection of the art of poetry, also entail a political function. They contribute, albeit indirectly, to the legitimation of absolutist power. Theater's new functional determination as an instrument for representing absolute power and for securing the renown of a great ruler necessitates its disconnection from the entertainment needs of a broad audience. The division of the audience into literary connoisseurs associated with the sphere of the court and a merely "look-happy" crowd [*schaulustige Menge*], the introduction of aesthetic evaluation oriented toward aristocratic norms of conduct, and the (later) changes in the generic framework of drama under the auspices of a generic hierarchy—all these changes cannot be explained in terms intrinsic to literature, even if we understand intrinsic literary evolution through its reception. The documents analyzed here show, rather, that the institutionalization of the *doctrine classique* has to do with a social dispute whose frontlines are indeed contradictory but can certainly be sorted out. On the one hand, we have the absolutist court's cultural program, which establishes rules as an instrument of the functional transformation of literature. On the other, we have the representatives of a theater dedicated to satisfying the entertainment needs of the "people." The parallel between this theater and ancient gladiator sports makes clear its role as distraction. The representatives of the nonnoble sector of the audience ("honnestes gens entre le peuple [the honest common people]" [Gasté, 231]) challenge the conscription of theater by a cultural program based on rational aesthetic norms, without being able as yet to offer a countermodel of their own (bourgeois) cultural program. Only at the beginning of the eighteenth century would Du Bois make "sentiment" the foundation of an egalitarian aesthetic, which the author of the *Jugement* was not able to do.[26] The hypothesis that the bourgeoisie in the first half of the seventeenth century were not yet in a position to become the bearers of an *independent* culture directed against the court seems plausible enough.

Corneille's Cid and the Material of Tragicomedy

In the first edition of *Le Cid*, Corneille calls the play a "tragicomédie." This generic designation is not accidental: it precisely indicates the artistic material that is Corneille's point of departure. In this section, we will first attempt to describe this material and to comprehend its historical character [*Gehalt*]. Following this, we will analyze *Le Cid* as an example for the reworking of this material. The historical character of the play, which is not the same as the author's intention, can be deduced above all from significant changes in the material of tragicomedy.[27]

As has been indicated, Corneille's *Cid* contains essential elements of the contemporary tragicomedy. If, however, *Le Cid* were only one of many contemporary tragicomedies, we would not be able to explain why one of the most important literary debates of the century was touched off by this play. In my view, it is precisely the changes in the material of tragicomedy that led to the success of the play and unleashed the subsequent debate. The changes can be demonstrated by comparing *Le Cid* with Rotrou's tragicomedy *Laure persecutée*, which was also performed in 1637.[28]

Rotrou's play also treats the reunion of a couple, the prince Orantée and Laure, descendent of an impoverished noble family. What separates the lovers is their unequal rank and the will of the king of Hungary, who wants his son Orantée to marry the infanta of Poland. As in *Le Cid*, the issue is a conflict about norms: the authority of the state as opposed to love. Each principle is embodied in a particular character: the king embodies the authority of the state and Orantée personifies love. More important, the conflict about norms represents only the denouement of the action. The action itself is driven by Octave, one of Orantée's *gentilhommes,* who plays the role of *traître*. Octave is in love with Laure, who has been promised to him by the king, provided he can win her love. Octave sets up a scene of deception to persuade Orantée of Laure's infidelity: Lydie, Laure's *confidente,* disguises herself as Laure and declares love to Octave; the king, who is aware of the deception, watches the scene, together with Orantée. The deception is completely successful; Orantée is persuaded of Laure's infidelity and experiences this betrayal as the total destabilization of the world (topos of the world turned up-side down).

Ah! ciel! ce n'est point toi qui régis la nature;
Tes astres impuissants errent à l'aventure;
La région du feu n'a point de pureté;
La terre, quoi qu'on die, est sans stabilité;
L'ombre produit les corps, et les corps suivent l'ombre
L'astre du jour est fixe, et sa lumière est sombre;
Le visage de Laure a de douteux appas,
Et rien n'est assuré, puisqu'elle ne l'est pas. (3.8)

[Oh, Heaven, it is not you who rules nature; / your impotent stars wander at random; / The realm of fire has lost its purity; / Whatever one says, the earth is without stability; / Darkness produces bodies, and bodies follow the darkness; the morning star is fixed and its light is sombre; / Laure's face has a doubtful charm, / and nothing is certain, because she is not.]

The rest of the scenes in the third act and the whole of the fourth act portray the stages of Orantée's despair. Not only does the world appear to him to have lost all stability, but he himself loses the ability to make decisions and act upon them. This condition is enacted in the "doubt" monologue typical of this genre. Orantée vacillates wildly between revenge plans ("De ma divinité ferai-je ma victime [Out of my divinity I will make my victim]") and love:

> Hélas! que résoudre-je en cette peine extrême?
> A peine je la hais que je l'aime. (3.11)

[Alas, how shall I resolve this extreme pain? / Hardly do I hate her than I love her again.]

At the beginning of the fourth act, we see Orantée standing outside Laure's house with his dagger drawn (suspense: will he kill Laure in a fit of jealousy? lyrical effect: apostrophe to her "beautiful door"). Orantée himself characterizes his state of mind as madness.

> Que veux-tu? sans dessein, sans conseil, sans conduite,
> Mon coeur, sollicité d'un invisible effort,
> Se laisse aveuglement attirer à son tort.
> Pour n'être pas témoin de ma folie extrême,
> Moi-même je voudrais être ici sans moi-même. (4.2)

[What do you want? Without plans, without counsel, without guidance, / My heart, summoned by an invisible force / Lets itself be pulled blindly in error. / So as not to be witness to my extreme madness, / I myself would prefer to be here without myself.]

It is important to clarify how the audience members would perceive this scene. They would see it in a double perspective: in the first place, they would be drawn to identify with Orantée's suffering and with the danger that he might kill himself in a moment of despair or Laure in a fit of jealousy; in the second, the audience knows that the suffering is only apparent, the result of the "traitor's" perfect deception. The audience can thus enjoy Orantée's confusion, because it is aware that it is only apparent and because the generic demands of the play entail a happy conclusion to all complications. The generic-specific dramaturgy of the *feinte* sets up a fictional threat. This is present (Orantée actually suffers) and can have actual consequences (hence the suspense), but *at the same time,* it is apparent (since the relationship between the two protagonists is in reality unimpaired).

After the deception is discovered (4.8), the fifth act can be devoted completely to the confirmation of happiness. Orantée himself articulates the aesthetic of tragicomedy:

> Enfin notre courage a vaincu toutes choses,
> Et parmi les soucis nous a trouvé des roses.
> La joie après l'ennui suit enfin notre espoir;
> Un beau matin nous luit après un triste soir,
> Et, parmi les effets de ces vicissitudes,
> Le sort a mis la fin à nos inquiétudes. (5.1)

> [At last our courage has conquered everything, / And, among our cares, found roses for us. / Joy, after our troubles, finally follows our hopes; / A beautiful morning after a sad evening, / And, amidst the effects of these vicissitudes, / Fate has put an end to our anxieties.]

In the final scene, Rotrou returns to the problem of norms in a rather ambiguous way. Laure presents her case (love across ranks) to the infanta, who decides unambiguously in favor of love and so also, without knowing it, against her marriage with Orantée:

> L'amour n'est point sujet au respect d'un parent;
> Il dépend de soi seul; cet enfant volontaire,
> Pour n'en point respecter, voulut naître sans père;
> Immortel, il posséde un absolu pouvoir,
> Et ne relève point de la loi du devoir.
> Donc, deux partis s'aimant en concourant ensemble

Au dessein que l'hymène sous ses lois les assemble,
Quelque inégalité qui divise leur sort,
L'amour étant égal doit être le plus fort,
Et, tout-puissant qu'il est, à son pouvoir suprême
Soumettre la fortune et la nature même. (5.8)

[Love is in no way subject to parental respect; / It depends on itself
alone; this willful child, / So as not to respect anyone, wanted to be
born without a father; / Immortal, he possesses an absolute power, /
And does not depend on the law of duty. / Thus, when two parties love
each other and both comply / With the plans of Hymen and his laws
bring them together, / and when some inequality divides their lots, /
Love being equal is the strongest, / And, all powerful as he is, compels
fortune and nature themselves to submit to his supreme power.]

This unmistakable judgment in favor of the rights of emotion, presented
here as egalitarian in the face of the hierarchy of a society based on rank,
is nonetheless relativized when Laure's noble birth is revealed. She is none
other than the sister of the infanta of Poland, and so the king can consent
to her marriage with Orantée. On the one hand, the law of the heart is elevated above existing distinctions of rank but, on the other, the revelation
of Laure's noble lineage reestablishes the social hierarchy that had been
questioned. The decision in favor of the egalitarian principle of the lovers'
self-determination is thus practically retracted as the object of the conflict
is removed (without knowing it, Laure and Orantée had after all chosen
partners of the appropriate rank). This ambiguous solution to the conflict
of norms is still present in the work of [Pierre de] Marivaux a century
later.[29] In the following analysis of *Le Cid*, we will return to the problem
of a sociohistorical interpretation of the pursuit of happiness articulated
in the infanta's judgment. For the moment, suffice it to say that Rotrou
attempts to satisfy different needs for self-assertion by the double solution
of the conflict between *amour* and *rang* [rank].

At the center of tragicomedy is pleasure in appearances, behind which
truth or deception may hide. In other words, tragicomedy takes up the
problematic of appearance and being [*Schein/Sein*] as the articulation of
an epochal experience of crisis. Without claiming to delineate the complex
economic, social, and political conditions of this experience of crisis, we

should nonetheless note that this problematic concretizes the destabilization of the norms of the period. In his social-psychological work on the emergence of modern France, Robert Mandrou has pointed to the ever-present anxiety as the social condition of the period, an anxiety which is grounded in the insufficient security of material existence and which is magnified by irrational notions of magic.[30] If we examine tragicomedy against the background of this kind of collective experience, we can formulate the hypothesis that this genre makes the motifs of anxiety and menace (the flaws of a normative order) into the object of pleasurable enjoyment. This transformation can occur because the appearance/being problematic is articulated not merely through the passive suffering of the characters but through the active mastery (of some) of reality. The audience's experience is a dual one: it can share the suffering of those deceived and *at the same time* admire the skill of the deceivers. The pleasure at the manipulability of appearance thus emerges out of the loss of normative orientation. As the threatening and deceptive qualities of human existence become the vehicles of strategic action, they acquire a manageable character. Although tragicomedy does not offer the audience a new normative order, it nonetheless represents the dominant disorder ("the labyrinth") as a product of human action. In this schema, the social-psychological function of tragicomedy becomes the elimination of anxiety.

This hypothesis also attempts to comprehend the extraordinary success of tragicomedy and related genres with a socially divided audience. The destabilization of current norms, already apparent in the religious wars, ought to be regarded as a basic experience for members of widely varying social classes and ranks in the urban population.

Before we examine the changes that Corneille intended to apply to contemporary tragicomic material, we ought first to look briefly at what they have in common. Antoine Adam has noted that *Le Cid* possesses "un thème particulièrement cher à la littérature romanesque [a theme particularly dear to romance literature]," namely, love between members of enemy clans.[31] Beyond this, there are at least two elements common to *Le Cid* and contemporary tragicomedy. We may note the prevalence of deception scenes. It is noteworthy that the two types of deception scenes typical of the contemporary theater appear in *Le Cid*: first, unintended deception, as when Don Sancho, having been defeated by Rodrigue in a duel, brings Chimène the latter's dagger and so unwittingly leads her to believe that Rodrigue has been killed (5.6); second, staged deception, such as the ruse that Don Fernand, like the theatrical kings of other plays, uses to establish whether Chimène loves Rodrigue (4.5). The similarities between Corneille's plays and contemporary tragicomedy are even more clearly demonstrated by the way in which the identity of the subject is developed in terms of the triad, love—separation—reunion, or, in the words of Orantée:

Enfin notre courage a vaincu toutes choses,
Et parmi les soucis nous a trouvé des roses

[At last our courage has conquered everything,
And, among our cares, found roses for us]   (*Laure* 5.1).

At this point, we come to the changes made by Corneille to the material of tragicomedy to which his play is so clearly indebted. Comparing *Le Cid* to Rotrou's *Laure persecutée*, we can see that Corneille's deception scenes have a different value from Rotrou's. Like the majority of contemporary comedies and tragicomedies, *Laure* is constructed on the basis of the opposition between appearance and being, illusion or deception and actuality. The love of the two protagonists is expressed in the realm of being, whereas the obstacles to this love are in the realm of appearance or illusion. Separating the lovers, on the one hand, is the *feinte* of the *traître;* on the other, the opposition between the values of *amour* and *rang*, which is finally revealed to be merely apparent. Whereas the development of the subject in Rotrou's tragicomedy is determined by the problematization of appearance and being and the corresponding centrality of the *feinte* and illusion motifs, the problematic of appearance and being is absent in *Le Cid* and so *feinte* and illusion are only episodic motifs.

Moreover, the structural schema based on the formula "from suffering to pleasure" is articulated differently in Corneille than in most tragicomedies of the period. The conflict of norms, whose function in *Laure* is only to resolve the plot whose complex structure captures the audience's attention, becomes the organizing center of the subject's development in Corneille. *Le Cid* is totally focused on the conflict between the values of *honneur* and *amour*.[32]

In Rotrou, the norms of state authority and love each have their representative character. The king represents the claims of state authority as rigidly as Orantée represents those of love. The dispute between them does not take the form of a careful deliberation of the relative justification of the different norms but, rather, makes use of violence (or the threat of violence) and deception. In Corneille, on the other hand, the conflict of norms is borne by the characters themselves. That is, the norms of interpersonal conduct are problematized. This can best be seen in the transformation of the "doubting" monologue typical of the genre. Rotrou's hero vacillates between two *feelings,* love and hate. The cause of his vacillation is a deception scene that persuaded him of Laure's alleged infidelity. Rodrigue vacillates between two *norms, honneur* and *amour* (see 1.6). The cause of his vacillation here is the dispute of the fathers, that is, the rivalry between two noble families. Orantée's complaint is focused exclusively on his own situation, whereas Rodrigue's articulates the normative contradiction.

The transformation of tragicomic material outlined here suggests that Corneille's play is not exhausted by the fulfillment of the social-psychological function of alleviating anxiety, which we have associated with tragicomedy. In departing from the appearance/being thematic and in problematizing norms of conduct, *Le Cid* can be seen as political theater in the broadest sense of the term. This claim requires proof that the norms dealt with in the play, especially the central value of honor, are still valid in the society of the time.[33] Indeed, the meaning which the feudal conception of honor had for the nobility of the period can be clearly seen in Richelieu's *Testament politique.* Richelieu criticizes not only "the barbaric custom whereby every injured man desires his own justice and his own satisfaction in the blood of his enemy."[34] He also carefully considers the appropriate means for limiting the current rage for dueling. In 1626 François Montmorency, who had apparently fought a duel on the Place Royale, was hanged with his second. Richelieu gave testimony to "the universal compassion for the unhappiness and the value of these young gentlemen, which struck at the heart of everyone" (*Testament,* 102). In the consciousness of the ruling social ranks influenced by the feudal value system ("Le Monde"), the duel was no crime, despite an ever-renewed ban on the practice. On the contrary, the ban had the effect of a provocation, because it provided not only the opportunity to defend one's honor against the injuring party but also to challenge the legal proscription (*Testament,* 224). Richelieu attacks duels with all available means, above all because dueling represents the clearest manifestation of feudal independence, which he wishes to destroy.[35]

Duels are also fought in contemporary plays in which battles are fought over honor. What distinguishes Corneille's treatment of the motif from the current procedure and makes his play political can be clarified with reference to Scudéry's *Le Prince déguisé*. As in *Le Cid*, the issue in *Le Prince* is the love between members of enemy clans. Cléarque, son of a king, wins the love of Argénie, another king's daughter, while disguised as a gardener. After their love is discovered, traditional custom would demand a duel to decide who is to live. Argénie, disguised as a knight, appears as Cléarque's champion, while Cléarque offers himself as Argénie's. Comparing this with *Le Cid*, we can see that only Corneille focuses on the real political character of the motif. In Scudéry, the lovers' reciprocal intervention for each other demonstrates the intensity of their love; in Corneille, the complicated casuistry of *honneur* is displayed in its most extreme consequences. We can say that in Corneille's hands tragicomic material rebounds on the social actuality of the time or, more precisely, on the prevailing normative conceptions.

This procedure corresponds to the procedure operating in Corneille's early comedies. In this case too, Corneille proceeds from the contemporary material but gives it a new actuality [*Wirklichkeitsgehalt*] by reversing, connecting, and transforming motifs. If Corneille's treatment of contemporary artistic material reveals similar traits in the early comedies and in *Le Cid*, then the discrepancy between the relatively limited success of the comedies and the extraordinary success of *Le Cid* requires an explanation. The reason for this discrepancy in the audience's response has above all to do with the increasingly evident tendency of Corneille's comedy toward the (bourgeois) problem play which would hold little interest for an audience influenced by prevailing aristocratic normative conceptions. *Le Cid*, on the other hand, disseminates and articulates those very prevailing conceptions. Insofar as the ideas of the rulers are most often also the ruling ideas (in Marx's formulation), the play's broad success becomes comprehensible.

Richelieu's evident hostility to the play ought also to be understood in this context. In general, the secondary literature treats the political tendency of the play as preabsolutist. Georges Couton, for example, summarizes his findings thus:

> As Corneille says in the interpretation of his tragicomedy, it is necessary to know how to forget familial revenge when the enemy is at the Somme. The lesson of *Le Cid* is an appeal to a sacred union. This appeal is accompanied by an invitation to forsake the duel. Corneille

ascertains that manners accept it. In law it remains regrettable and politically dangerous because it can be extended into civil war. It is desirable that a new law be established and that the cult of a point of honor give way to the superior interest of the realm, to the reason of state. Ideologically speaking, the play was able to satisfy the Cardinal.[36]

Likewise Wolfgang Mittag, who thoroughly examines the antiabsolutist moments in Rodrigue's conduct, to which we will return, stresses that Rodrigue submits to the king.[37]

Je sais trop que je dois au bien de votre empire
Et le sang qui m'anime, et l'air que je respire;
Et quand je les perdrai pour un si digne objet,
Je ferai seulement de devoir d'un sujet.

[I know too well the debt I owe your reign,
The blood that fires me and the air I breathe,
And, when I lose them for so bold an aim,
I only do a subject's duty, Sire.]   (4.3.1233ff.)[38]

Both interpretations focus on important moments in the play. Every attempt to read an antiabsolutist tendency in the text would doubtless be false. Yet it ought to be possible to comprehend Richelieu's "persecution" of *Le Cid*, of which Chapelain speaks in political terms. This seems to me possible if we distinguish between the explicit assent to absolutism expressed in the play and the implicit political character of the play. The latter can be deduced above all from the actions of the protagonists and their normative grounding. The object of the audience's emotional involvement was presumably both protagonists. Rodrigue's actions—above all, the duel as well as the attack on the Moors undertaken without royal command—clearly follow feudal norms of conduct.[39] Further, Rodrigue does not cast any doubt on the validity of these norms. He must kill the count in order to restore the honor of his family.

Car enfin n'attends pas de mon affection
Un lâche repentir d'une bonne action.

[For in a word do not expect of me
Craven repentence for a rightful deed.]   (3.4.871ff.)

The conflict between the norms of *honneur* and *amour* which Rodrigue expresses in the famous line "Contre mon propre honneur mon amour s'interesse [Against my honour, love takes up arms]" (1.6.302ff.; trans. modified), he later resolves unambiguously in favor of the feudal hierarchy of values, according to which the realization of other values is dependent on the primary value of *honneur*. Dishonored, Rodrigue would have also lost Chimène's love: "Qu'un homme sans honneur ne te méritait pas; . . . Qui m'aima généreux me hairait infâme [That I, dishonoured, did not merit you; . . . Who loved me brave would hate me infamous]" (3.4.888ff.). Chimène, too, whose relationship to the feudal code of honor needs further examination, does not challenge its validity:

Ah! Rodrigue! il est vrai, quoique ton ennemie,
Je ne puis te blâmer d'avoir fui l'infamie; . . .
De quoi qu'en ta faveur notre amour m'entretienne,
Ma générosité doit répondre à la tienne:
Tu t'es, en m'offensant, montré digne de moi;
Je me dois, par ta mort, montrer digne de toi.

[Rodrigo. Ah! it's true. Although your foe,
I cannot blame your "No" to infamy. . . .
Whate'er our love may plead on your behalf,
My noble-heartedness must equal yours.
By wronging me you're worthy of my hand.
I must be worthy of you by your death.]   (3.4.905f., 929ff.)

While the protagonists, on whom the audience's attention is focused, think through the feudal honor code to its murderous consequences, the absolutist counterposition is represented only by secondary characters who can hardly lay claim to the spectator's interest. A courtier, Don Arias, represents the fundamental principles of absolutism against the count, who is still thoroughly saturated by feudal high-handedness (see 2.1). As regards the king, Don Ferdinand, Corneille notes his weakness as early as the *Examen*: "la manière dont ce dernier agit, qui ne parait pas assez vigoureuse [the way in which the latter acts does not appear to be vigorous enough]." More precisely, he does not act but is, rather, presented with the fact of others' actions. This is the case for the duel between the count and Rodrigue as well as for Rodrigue's attack on the Moors. Where the king does act, in staging the deception that is supposed to expose Chimène's love, his action resembles that of the theater kings of contemporary tragicomedy.

Moreover, the victorious Rodrigue's acknowledgment of the king's absolute power departs significantly from the political theory of the period, as Wolfgang Mittag has shown. It is an "act of self-determination."[40] Rodrigue freely chooses to submit to the king. Thus the principle of absolutism is transformed into its polar opposite. The king's claim to power comes to depend on the voluntary submission of the powerful feudal nobility. It should be clear that the implicit political character of the play was certainly likely to displease Richelieu. This does not imply that Corneille wanted to write a play that would glorify feudal norms, but only that Richelieu was able to find the play politically explosive. Werner Krauss explains Richelieu's reaction thus:

> In *Le Cid*, an appealing image of life emerged in the hues of heroic inheritance. It had to touch the buried feelings of masses of people who had unwillingly borne the yoke of political reason and who continually awaited the call to passionate rebellion. To be sure, the situation of the past civil wars had been eliminated, but it had given life to a generation growing up in tumultuous circumstances, who instinctively resisted any form of order. Hence the political substance that concealed the core of the state had to arouse counterforces, and the magic of Corneille's poetry could not but provoke dangerous illusions. At least, that was the Cardinal's view, as he foresaw the furthest consequences of uncontrolled stimulation.[41]

The *querelle du Cid* documents demonstrate that the play was well received by all sections of a strongly differentiated audience. At first glance, this fact appears to challenge the dominance of the feudal normative conceptions examined here. For, one could ask, what in the feudal code of honor could interest the nonnoble audience members? This argument depends on an all-too-simple model of analysis, which attempts to draw parallels between works and groups of works and particular social ranks and classes. Nonetheless, we should concede that there is a problem here. I suggest the following solution: either evidence must be sought that the normative character of the play was also valid for the nonnoble ranks, or the play must be shown to contain other (nonfeudal) normative elements that might explain the interest of the bourgeois audience members. We will examine both possibilities.

The broad success of a play whose normative character is so clearly feudal yet in no way limited to a noble audience can be understood if we recall that up to the Fronde the nobility undoubtedly possessed a normative power that also constrained other social ranks. The social historian Robert Mandrou speaks of the "mimeticism which the dominant class created around itself: the nobility of the sword." The feudal concept of honor, he suggests, found some expression in all other classes and groups and even in written rules as well as everyday practice as regulated by custom. Every social group developed its own concept of honor. This was true even for highway robbers.[42] In light of these social historical findings, *Le Cid*'s success with the nonnoble as well as noble audience becomes comprehensible. If all social groups adopt the feudal concept of honor and reformulate it to fit their own social practice, then they could all recognize their own problems in the conflict of norms in *Le Cid*.

This explanation outlined here does, one must concede, limit our access to the second interpretive possibility mentioned above. For, if the normative power of the nobility predominates, we would have to play down the attempt to attribute the play's success with nonnoble audience members to potentially "bourgeois" moments in the text. Nonetheless, the question arises whether the normative character of Corneille's play is exhausted by the dissemination of feudal normative conceptions or whether there are other normative elements to be found in the play which contradict feudal norms.

At this point, we should look at the character of Chimène, who, as we have seen, provoked hostile criticism as an unnatural daughter [*fille dénaturée*] from the first. For Scudéry, Chimène is immodest [*impudique*] because, in loving Rodrigue, she loves her father's murderer.[43] Serge Doubrovsky reiterates the condemnation of the character by blaming her for being inconsistent in her pursuit of heroic self-realization: "Chimène would like to follow [Rodrigue's] example, but she cannot; in her the heroic dialectic runs awry. She remains caught, ensnared by passion. . . . at the stage of desire, unable to seek contentment beyond tangible loss; instead of eradicating or sacrificing her love, she is infected by it; she cannot transcend the realm of the body."[44]

Doubrovsky stands completely on the side of feudal *honneur*, which he understands in terms of the abstract existentialist concept of freedom as the means of self-realization. According to this interpretation, Chimène remains trapped in the lower sphere of instinctive drives (*désir, règne vital*), incapable of reaching the higher sphere of self-determination through self-overcoming. Precisely because Doubrovsky's study represents one of the most significant recent interpretive essays on Corneille, his facile attempt to reinterpret the feudal ethos in existentialist terms is truly astonishing. Fixated on the abstract "dialectic of heroes" (self-realization through self-overcoming), he misunderstands those moments in the play in which the overcoming of the feudal concept of honor is implied. We have seen that the king only incompletely embodies the historically new. Chimène's case is different. In the first encounter with Rodrigue after the count's death, she notes the match between Rodrigue's action and the dominant norms and announces her desire to conduct herself according to the same norms. At the same time, however, she acknowledges that *honneur* and *devoir* are beyond her. The obligation to avenge her father is for her "un affreux devoir [a terrible duty]" (3.4.925). Just beforehand, she had already confessed: "Je demande sa tête, et crais de l'obtenir [I demand his head, and fear to receive it]" (3.3.827). Revenge is for her only an outward obligation which she has to fulfill because of her social standing: "Je sais ce que je suis, et que mon père est mort [I know who I am and that my father is dead]" (3.3.824). As a feeling individual she takes Rodrigue's side ("Mon coeur prend son parti"). In contrast to Rodrigue, who adopts the feudal ethos after hesitating briefly and thus realizes himself through it, Chimène's character is marked by a dissociation of individual and social role.

> Si jamais je t'aimai, cher Rodrigue, en revanche,
> Défends-toi maintenant pour m'ôter à don Sanche;
> Combats pour m'affranchir d'une condition
> Qui me donne à l'objet de mon aversion.
> Te dirai-je encor plus? va, songe à ta défense,
> Pour forcer mon devoir, pour m'imposer silence;
> Et si tu sens pour moi ton coeur encore épris,
> Sors vainqueur d'un combat dont Chimène est le prix.
> Adieu: ce mot lâche me fait rougir de honte.

> [If ever, dear, I loved you, in return,
> Fight back to save me from Don Sancho now.
> Release me from a grim predicament
> Which gives me to a man whom I abhor.
> Need I say more? Go, think of your defence,

To force my duty and to silence me;
And, if you love me, come victorious from
A fight for which Chimène is the prize.
Farewell. I blush with shame at having spoken thus.]

(5.1.1549–57; trans. modified)

It is important to remember that the untragic outcome of the play, that is, the conquest of the feudal concept of honor, is directly dependent on the separation of subject and institutionalized role playing. Measured against the feudal concept of honor, Chimène's behavior seems to suggest weakness or attachment to the lower sphere of physical needs; it can also be treated (albeit cautiously) as modern subjectivity. In this view, Chimène is the character that prevents *Le Cid* from becoming a mere document of feudal norms. What, in Doubrovsky's opinion, is censured as Chimène's incapacity for heroic self-realization, can be seen as the expression of a historically new type of human self-realization; this type does not yet openly attack the dominant normative order but at least attempts to dissociate itself from that order.

Based on the interpretation of Chimène sketched here, we can say that the play not only represents feudal norms but also problematizes them to a certain degree. Thus the high-handed behavior of Don Gormas, which can rightly be seen as a representation of the old feudal nobility's mode of conduct, is sharply repudiated in several scenes because it contradicts the notion of absolute monarchy. At issue here is the discussion and problematization of norms. Certainly, this problematization of norms is nothing new; nonetheless, we ought at least to consider whether this constitutes a modern moment in the play. Norms in traditional societies tend to be rigidly fixed; only in modern (bourgeois) society do they become reflexive and susceptible to discussion and critique. The way in which norms are treated in *Le Cid* and in other plays by Corneille occupies a middle ground. On the one hand, the protagonists continually reinforce the validity of the feudal hierarchy of values which grants *honneur* the highest place; on the other hand, the outcome of the play undermines the obligation of reciprocal revenge, while the conduct of Chimène treats *honneur* as a merely external value and thus challenges its validity.

We ought at this point to specify the significance of this interpretation of Chimène as well as the arguments associated with it. We should be aware that the categories of traditional and modern normative conceptions represent only a crude grid on which to situate Corneille. Something else is more important: the above outline presupposes the complete development of modern reflexive normative conceptions. That also means that this interpretation is possible only with the evolution of bourgeois society. There is a general consensus in the theoretical realm that the character of literary works is not fixed for all time but undergoes historical transformation, which in the final analysis harks back to social transformation. It is nonetheless very difficult to organize our interpretive practice around this insight. We still tend toward that which we recognize in a work, rather than focusing on its true character. Instead, we ought to acknowledge that social change and changes in the institutionalization of literature make it possible for us to recognize other moments in past works.

We have interpreted Chimène's conduct as a break with the feudal norm of *honneur*. Is this conduct to be understood as bourgeois? The question is also relevant in the case of the infanta's judgment in Rotrou's *Laure persecutée*, which openly expresses the lower orders' claim to personal happiness. Proceeding from the fact that the eighteenth-century bourgeoisie treated happiness as one of their central values, we can argue for a bourgeois moment in this claim for self-realization through love against feudal concepts of honor and social hierarchy. Yet this interpretation is problematic insofar as it transplants characteristics of the prerevolutionary bourgeoisie into the different context of the first half of the seventeenth century.

To make the question more precise: do the modes of conduct at issue here correspond to the understanding of norms by the bourgeoisie of the 1630s? We cannot go into the controversial sociohistorical question of whether we can talk of the seventeenth-century bourgeoisie as a class with a developed class consciousness.[45] If we proceed from Mandrou's description, we can distinguish certain characteristic features of the seventeenth-century bourgeoisie: a certain way of life distinct from that of the nobility or the lower social ranks and based on the social security provided by property; a mentality that includes prudence, thrift, a sense of profit and expenditure, and a certain luxury; finally, a self-perception based on a distinction between themselves and manual workers designated *vil peuple* [common people].[46] It is clear that this bourgeoisie cannot be the bearer of the demands for self-realization through passion which were inescapably present in the infanta's judgment in *Laure* and Chimène's lament in

Le Cid. Likewise, the attendant idea that this demand for happiness gave voice to the needs of the lower social ranks cannot be substantiated. The notion that these ranks were the least affected by the prevailing norms and were thus capable of articulating individual claims to happiness can only be a romantic view. Research on seventeenth-century popular culture has highlighted its total conformity to prevailing norms.[47] In this context the nonnormative desire for happiness, for freedom to live in love, can equally be understood as a feudal value.[48] The conflict between *rang* and *amour* in Rotrou and between *honneur* and *amour* in Corneille thus becomes an internal conflict within the feudal system of norms.

Does this mean that the interpretation of Chimène's conduct as a break with an unconditional submission to the primacy of *honneur* is untenable? I think not; it is only revealed for what it is: an interpretation from a later (bourgeois) perspective. If these reflections are apt, then we can say that this interpretation of Chimène's character cannot be retrospectively projected onto the original period of the play. Only later, in developed bourgeois society, once literature has become the means of reflection on the possibilities and limits of human self-realization in society, can the character of Chimène become the central point of an interpretation of *Le Cid.*

Notes

1. Hans-Georg Gadamer, *Wahrheit und Methode. Grundzüge einer philosophischen Hermeneutik* (Tübingen, 1965), 289; translated as *Truth and Method* (New York: Continuum, 1975).
2. These remarks are not directed in general against attempts to make past literature contemporary but only against unmediated attempts, as should be clear from my other work. By unmediated [*unreflektiert*], I mean an appropriation of the work that ignores the historical distance that separates the work from the interpreter, or an appropriation that presupposes tradition and the inherited canon instead of problematizing their historicization. A work is not accessible to present-day appropriation merely because it is in the canon; the issue of the time and manner of its appropriation is a significant question for literary scholarship. See Peter Bürger, *Aktualität und Geschichtlichkeit. Studien zum gesellschaftlichen Funktionswandel der Literatur* (Frankfurt, 1977), especially the introduction, "Zum Problem der Aneignung literarischer Werke

der Vergangenheit," and the first section of the Stendhal essay, which treats the false opposition between unmediated appropriation and historicism.

3. See P. Bürger, *Aktualität*, 9ff.

4. "In the analysis of literary evolution we find the following steps: (1) the dialectical emergence of a new construction principle in contrast to the automatized construction principle; (2) the new principle is applied; (3) it is further disseminated, becomes a mass phenomenon; (4) it becomes automatic and so provokes a new construction principle" (Juri Tynjanov, "Das literarische Faktum," in his *Die literarische Kunstmittel und die Evolution in der Literatur* [Frankfurt, 1967], 21).

5. See Peter Bürger, "Neoformalismus und Hermeneutik," in his *Vermittlung—Rezeption—Funktion* (Frankfurt, 1979).

6. See E. Kohler's proposed solution to this problem of literary evolution: "Gattungssystem und Gesellschaftssystem," *Romanistische Zeitschrift für Literaturgeschichte* 1 (1977): 7–22, as well as the work of his student: H. Krauss, "Zum 'dolce stil nuovo.' Dichtung einer Schicht zwischen der Schichten," in *Sprachen der Lyrik. Festschrift für Hugo Friedrich zum 70. Geburtstag*, ed. E. Kohler (Frankfurt, 1975), 447–86; D. Rieger, "Gattungstradition und historisch-soziale Realität. Mme de Lafayettes 'Zayde' im Kontext des französischen Romans des 17. Jahrhunderts," *Germanisch-Romanische Monatsschrift*, n.s. 26 (1976): 406–27.

7. See Peter Bürger, "The Institution of Art as a Category of the Sociology of Literature," in this volume.

8. Gustave Lanson, *Histoire de la littérature française* (Paris, 1901), 418.

9. Ibid., 419.

10. Antoine Adam, *Histoire de la littérature française au XVIIe siècle* (Paris, 1962), 1:516.

11. See Jean Chapelain, *Lettres*, ed. Philippe Tamizey de Larroque (Paris, 1880), 1:159.

12. Ibid.

13. See Peter Bürger, *Die frühen Komödien Pierre Corneilles und das französische Theater um 1630* (Frankfurt, 1971), chap. 1.

14. H. J. Martin, *Livre, pouvoirs et société à Paris au XVIIe siècle* (Geneva, 1969), 289.

15. A. Gasté, ed., *La Querelle du Cid. Pièces et pamphlets* (1898; repr., Geneva, 1970), 64 (hereafter, Gasté).

16. Georges de Scudéry, *Ligdamon et Lidias ou la ressemblance*, tragicomedy (Paris, 1631), n.p.

17. Chapelain, *Lettres* 1:135.

18. As Tallemant de Réaux reports: "The Cardinal does not appreciate the fact that he [Balzac] dedicated neither his *Prince* nor his letters to the Cardinal" (*Historiettes*, ed. Antoine Adam [Paris, 1960–61], 2:43–46).

19. Georges de Scudéry, "A Madame de Combalet," in his *Le Trompeur puni ou l'histoire septentrionale*, tragicomedy (Paris, 1635), n.p.; "ce Criminel" is an allusion to the anonymous hero of the play.

20. Chapelain describes the "Cour" as an audience category in a letter to Balzac: "That is the name I give to those delicate ears and those who judge things as you do" (Chapelain, *Lettres* 1:251).

21. See Scudéry's "Au lecteur," prefacing *Le Prince déguisé* (Paris, 1636): "But when this sweet illusion is dissipated and one perceives the deception and finally when judgment retrieves the freedom of its faculty, one no longer sees what one thought one saw: one mocks the work and oneself, and one's earlier ill-founded admiration changes to just disdain."

22. See P. Bürger, *Die frühen Komödien Pierre Corneilles*, 87ff.

23. That the rules of the *doctrine classique* are still treated as transhistorical in the teaching of literature is clear in the school edition of *Le Cid* (Paris, 1972), in which the infanta is once again treated as superfluous.

24. See Martin, *Livre, pouvoirs et société à Paris au XVIIe siècle*, 289, 1077. The ways in which the audience's entertainment needs were met after the institutionalization of rules cannot concern us here. A reference to opera and "pièces à machines" will have to suffice. We might also want to investigate the persistence of tragicomic techniques within tragedy.

25. Chapelain, *Lettres* 1:90.

26. See Peter Bürger, "Zur Auffassung des Publikums bei Du Bos und Desfontaines," in his *Studien zur französischen Frühaufklärung* (Frankfurt, 1972), 44–68.

27. I return here to the same procedure that I used in the book on Corneille, which placed a greater emphasis on Corneille's originality. For further discussion, see my comments on *feinte* (80ff.), the dialectic between appearance and being (106ff.), the "doubting" monologue (190ff.).

28. In Rotrou, *Théâtre choisi*, ed. F. Hémon, Classiques Garnier (Paris, 1925), 148–213. All further references to the play are to this edition; numbers refer to act and scene.

29. See H. J. Neuschäfer, "Die Evolution der Gesellschaftsstruktur im französischen Theater des 18. Jahrhunderts," *Romanische Forschungen* 82 (1970): 516ff., and Peter Bürger, "Herr und Knecht bei Marivaux," in his *Studien zur französischen Frühaufklärung*, 148f.

30. R. Mandrou, *Introduction à la France moderne (1500–1640). Essai de psychologie historique* (Paris, 1974), 324ff.

31. Adam, *Histoire de la littérature française* 1:509.

32. Since Charles Péguy's interpretation of Corneille, it has become commonplace to point out that this conflict is an illusory conflict, since even Chimène could not accept a disinherited Rodrigue as a partner, and hence no hesitation was possible. To be sure, the old feudal conception of norms, which included a

clear hierarchy of values and treated *honneur* as the highest, is correctly described by Péguy, but Corneille's drama, which at least partially problematizes this conception, is misrepresented. See Serge Doubrovsky's critique of Péguy's interpretation in *Corneille et la dialectique du héros* (Paris, 1963), 99ff.

33. See Georges Couton, *Réalisme de Corneille* (Paris, 1953).

34. Richelieu, *Testament politique*, ed. A. André and L. Noel (Paris, 1947), 225 (hereafter, *Testament*).

35. Richelieu characterized the situation before his tenure thus: "les grands se conduisoient comme s'ils n'eussent pas été ses sujets, et les plus puissants Gouverneurs des Provinces comme s'ils eussent été souverains en leurs charges [the nobility behaved as though they were not subjects (of the king), and the most powerful provincial governors as though they owed no allegiance to anyone except themselves]" (*Testament*, 93). ✓

36. Couton, "La Pensée politique de Pierre Corneille," in *Europe* 540–41 (1974): 60.

37. Wolfgang Mittag, "Individuum und Staat im dramatischen Werk Pierre Corneilles" (Ph.D. diss., University of Münster, 1976), 185ff.

38. Pierre Corneille, "Le Cid," in *Théâtre complet*, ed. Georges Couton (Paris, 1971), vol. 1; trans. John Cairncross, *The Cid, Cinna, and the Theatrical Illusion* (Harmondsworth, 1980); further references to the play cite this translation unless otherwise indicated; numbers refer to act, scene, and lines.

39. See the pioneering study of Pierre Bénichou, *Morales du grand siècle*, Collection Idées, 143 (Paris, 1967), chaps. 1 and 2.

40. Mittag, "Individuum und Staat," 186.

41. Werner Krauss, *Corneille als politischer Dichter* (Marburg, 1936), 16.

42. Mandrou, *Introduction à la France moderne*, 327.

43. Georges de Scudéry, "Observations sur le Cid," in Gasté, 80.

44. Doubrovsky, *Corneille et la dialectique du héros*, 110.

45. See the dispute between B. Porchnev, in *Les Soulèvements populaires en France au XVIIe siècle* (Paris, 1972), and R. Mousnier, *Les Hiérarchies sociales de 1450 à nos jours* (Paris, 1969).

46. Mandrou, *Introduction*, 151ff.

47. Mandrou writes, "Finally, and above all, popular cultures imply an acceptance of society as it is and thus a conformism which leaves no room for contestation, however slight it may be" (*La France aux XVIIe et XVIIIe siècles* [Paris, 1967], 145).

48. See also Pierre Bénichou's remark: "Aristocratic society has never allowed for restraint of passion as a condition of human value" (*Morales du grand siècle*, 21).

3.

Problems in
the Functional
Transformation
of Art and Literature
during the Transition
from Feudal to
Bourgeois Society

Literary History as History of the
Functional Transformation of Literature

Instead of "literary history as historical task," the watchword for West German literary scholarship after 1945 was the "work of art in language" [*das sprachliche Kunstwerk*].[1] Werner Krauss's programmatic essay, "Literaturgeschichte als geschichtlicher Auftrag [Literary history as historical task]" (1950), made the critique of traditional literary scholarship the precondition for a renewal of literary history. This essay, which deployed the insights of the young Marx on the interconnectedness of individual and society, went largely unnoticed in the West.[2] West German scholarship meanwhile adopted the New Critical view of literature which privileged the immanent perspective on literature. The "contemplation on the essence of a poetic work of art" allowed scholars to repress the Nazi moment of their own discipline, while cutting off any question about the historicity of the literary work.[3] The problem of literary history was so thoroughly repressed from literary scholarship that Hans Robert Jauss could describe his proposal for a reception-aesthetic renewal of literary history as a provo-

This outline is part of a project initiated by myself and the economist Gerhart Leithäuser and supported by the Central Research Commission of the University of Bremen: "Literature as Institution: On the Historical Transformation of the Social Function of Literature." Thanks to the collaborators on this project, Onno Frels and Bernd Passer, as well as colleagues, Lother Paul, Hans Sanders, and Gert Sautermeister.

cation, even though his central thesis was only a reformulation of the formalist theory of literary evolution.[4]

Attempts to establish the historicity of literary works in the two decades after 1945 were undertaken above all by the great Hegelian Marxists, Georg Lukács and Theodor Adorno. The polemic between Lukács and Adorno, which was motivated politically (by the cold war) and aesthetically (by their divergent valuations of the avant-garde), obscured the commonalities of their positions for a long time. The central issue for both is the illumination of individual works against a background of a relatively general conception of the history of bourgeois society. Adorno especially focuses almost exclusively on interpretation which renders the work contemporary, against which literary history looks like the alienated treatment of literature.[5] The question of the social function of literature, meanwhile, is not absolutely erased but is hardly a theme of Adorno's work. This point ought to return us to the fact that Lukács and Adorno retained an affiliation—although in different ways—to German idealism and so to a certain functional determination of art.[6] In other words, for Lukács and Adorno, the creations of the European avant-garde movements—whether marked negatively (Lukács) or positively (Adorno)—are still *works* that can be described and interpreted according to aesthetic categories. In contrast, Walter Benjamin tried, on the basis of an analysis of the changes in the production and reception of art by the techniques of mass reproduction, to effect a radical break in the evolution of art in bourgeois society at the beginning of the twentieth century.[7] However one may judge Benjamin's theses on their own, what remains is the achievement of his theoretical examination of the avant-garde's attempted break with what advanced bourgeois society calls "art" and thus his thematization of the problem of art's functional transformation.[8]

Developments in France have been different from those in West Germany. In France, literary scholarship in the wake of Gustave Lanson maintained an interest (albeit rather narrow, historically) in literary history. Along with several articles in the *Revue d'Histoire Littéraire de la France*, one should note Antoine Adam's monumental history of seventeenth-century French literature.[9] In light of this tradition of historicopositivist literary scholarship, which survived into the 1960s and even weathered the arrival of the so-called *nouvelle critique*, Roland Barthes's essay "Histoire ou littérature?" takes on particular significance.[10]

Barthes critiques literary history for being a succession of monographs on individual authors. Even if many literary histories examine genres and schools, the author and his work are always in the center: "At best, literary history is still the history of works." [11] Barthes objects to the fact that traditional literary history does not communicate historical knowledge but deals instead in [journalistic] literary criticism [*Literaturkritik*]. He argues rather for a strict distinction between "literary institution" and "literary creation." By "literary institution" Barthes means the determining conditions of the production and reception of literature in a given epoch or period. He names the following particular areas of investigation: (1) an examination of the writer's milieu, which he understands as the "area of habits of thought, implicit taboos, 'natural' value, the material interests of a group of people, which are concretely linked by identical or complementary functions, in short: a cross section of a social class";[12] (2) a historicosociological analysis of the audience, its social composition, and its notions of literature: "what interests us more than the sociological composition are questions like: what function does theater have in their eyes? distraction? dream? identification? distance? snobbery?"; lastly, examinations of the "intellectual evolution of this audience and its authors." [13]

The value of these studies that Barthes suggests is not disputable. What is particularly valuable is first the attention to the writer as member of a social class, for historical research in the context of a focus on the individual author all too easily serves the interests of an auratic worship of the "poet." Further, one ought to recognize that Barthes understands the audience's attitude of reception as a form of social conduct and does not focus, in the matter of reception aesthetics, exclusively on the experience of literary works. Nonetheless, this stance is methodologically problematic, because Barthes too sharply separates the historical research of the limit conditions of literary production and reception in a bygone period from the appropriation of individual literary works: a historically conceived history of the institution of literature from the hermeneutically informed interpretation of works, singly or in groups. Barthes's conception of these separate disciplines does not allow for mutual illumination. The interpretation of individual works remains tied to the (usually hidden) premises of the interpreter, whereas the history of the literary institution does not yield any arguments for or against any interpretation. That, however, is exactly what is needed. If the illumination of the present and the illumination of the past are intertwined in a historical-hermeneutic field of study,[14] the dissociation of a historically informed account of the literary institution can be remedied. This endeavor is interesting not merely as such but first of all as a necessary corrective of individual interpretations and also as a contribution to the clarification of the historical conditions of current notions of literature (including those that guide the interpreter). The task of a critical hermeneutics must be to develop concepts that do not rigidly juxtapose the limit conditions of the production and reception of literature with individual works but, rather, demonstrate that the functional transformation of literature and the succession of individual works are part of *one* historical process.

The discussion so far leads us to two demands on the concept of the institution of art or literature: (1) Only reflection on the historicity of the category allows it to be defined so as to avoid the illusion of objectivism, or the notion that scholars and their investigation are outside the institution that they are attempting to grasp. I have attempted to develop this category of the institution of art/literature in the *Theory of the Avant-garde*. (2) The category must contain concepts that establish the context on the level of the individual work. This is the issue discussed in my essay "Institution of Art as a Category of the Sociology of Literature," in which the concepts of *aesthetic norm* and *artistic material* ensure the connection between the institution and the individual work.[15] The issue here is not to reiterate the results of this research but instead to clarify the practical research value of the category "institution of art" for the comprehension of the functional transformation of art and literature. Changes in the institutionalization of art and literature during the transition from feudal to bourgeois society will be examined in the light of exemplary texts that thematize the social function of art. In this way the interconnectedness of general notions of art (functional determinations), aesthetic norms, and attitudes of reception can be elaborated and the sociohistorical conditions of the various institutionalizations of art can be made clear. Commentary on individual texts in aesthetic theory clearly do not replace a functional history of literature but, rather, highlight its necessity.[16]

The Enlightenment-Bourgeois Institution of Art/Literature

One of the [French] Encyclopedists' essential concerns is to revaluate the "mechanical arts" against the "liberal arts" [*freie Künste*]. Although this opposition is not the same as that between manual and intellectual labor, many of their speculations tend in this direction. They ground the re-valuation of the "mechanical arts" in their social *utility*. Beyond that is the insight that material production represents the decisive condition for social development and thus also for intellectual work. More concretely, the revaluation of the "mechanical arts" can be read as an expression of the interests of the manufacturing bourgeoisie in technological progress. Proceeding from these notions, we can consider two concepts of art: the "fine arts" [*schöne Künste*] can either be disposed of as a medium of mere pleasure, occupying a relatively low place in the system of human knowledge, or the attempt can be made to subject them to the universal utility principle. Both propositions are formulated in the *Encyclopédie*: the first in d'Alembert's *Discours préliminaire*, the second in the article on *beaux arts*.

> Among the liberal arts, the "fine arts" [*beaux arts*] are those whose aim is the imitation of nature and which serve to delight us. They are distinguished not only in this way from the necessary or useful arts such as grammar, logic, and morality. The latter have fixed and immutable rules that each can adopt from the others without further ado. The exercise of the fine arts, on the other hand, involves invention, which owes its principles to genius. The written rules of these arts only affect their mechanical side and fulfill the function of a telescope: they are useful only for those who can see.[17]

D'Alembert distinguishes between "fine arts" and "necessary and useful liberal arts" in two ways: in the first case, the function of the fine arts is to delight; in the second, they obey no firm and unchanging rules. To be sure, necessity is also stressed in the normative poetics of the court [*höfische Regelpoetik*], the poet must possess *génie*, but that is not crucial for the writing of poetry that presents itself as a construction according to rules that can be learned. In opposition to the normative poetics of the court, d'Alembert grants rules only minor significance as mechanical tools. Read in isolation, the above passage could be seen as an anticipation of Kant's proposition that genius is a talent "for creating something that does not conform to any particular rules, rather than a clever construction which can be learned according to the rules."[18] The crucial difference between d'Alembert and Kant lies in their respective valuations of "fine art." Whereas Kant praises artistic activity by sharply distinguishing it from aptitude or craft, d'Alembert treats the lack of rational rules that can be learned and the functional determination of what delights us as the occasion for a rather negative evaluation. That arises from the fact that the Encyclopedists treat social utility as the highest value. D'Alembert's text makes clear that in the middle of the eighteenth century the "fine arts" have already fallen from the ranks of technical and scientific, rationally grounded activities, without being set crudely against this realm.

The article on *beaux arts* [fine art] in the *Encyclopédie* is to be understood as the systematic attempt to confront these tendencies toward autonomy on the part of "fine art." The writer explicitly challenges the perception that "fine arts" function only to stimulate the senses and the imagination, and thus also attacks art's function as diversion: "Les esprits foibles ou frivoles répètent sans cesse que les *beaux arts* ne sont destinés qu'à nos amusements; que leur but ne vas pas plus loin qu'à récréer nos sens et notre imagination [Weak or frivolous minds are constantly repeating that the *fine arts* are intended only to amuse us, and that their purpose is only to delight our senses and our imagination]." [19] Against the argument for amusement, the writer emphasizes the social utility of art. We should not treat utility as an essential attribute of the "fine arts." It arises rather out of life-praxis: the shepherd decorates his staff with wood carving; the savage builds himself a well-proportioned hut and finds an example, or better—a stimulus—in nature: "une beauté qui est indépendente de son utilité [beauty which is independent of its utility]." Beauty is an attribute of the works of creation, which does not coincide with their utility. Nonetheless, at the same time a moral purpose is attributed to natural beauty: the strengthening of a "gentle sensitivity" [*douce sensibilité*] which mitigates passion and selfishness.

The intention of the author is obviously to legitimate "fine arts" in social terms by demonstrating their utility. In order to comprehend this intention we must recall that, for the courtly-feudal society, art functioned above all as *divertissement* and [social] representation. For the bourgeoisie intent on the utility principle, the battle against a notion that reduced the function of art to that of entertainment (*amusement*) is above all a battle against a courtly, that is, aristocratic notion of art.[20]

Nonetheless it would be wrong to attribute the instrumentalization of art for moral ends exclusively to an attack on the courtly-feudal institution of art. Some passages in the article reveal that the author suspects a potential in art which ought to be kept under control. The response to the question of what distinguishes the recitation of a poem from the movement of a dance is blunt: the essence of the fine arts lies in the "peculiar charm" (*charme particulier*) of the work. At another point he speaks of its "magical power" (*force magique*). One would not want to overemphasize these remarks but they do suggest that the Enlighteners also saw in art the impact of irrational power; hence their proposals for a restricted politics of art. They particularly stressed the possibility that the "fine arts" might exercise a fateful influence because they addressed the senses: "It is one and the same sensuousness that creates heroes and madmen, saints and criminals." This argument leads the writer to draw the conclusion that the political powers that be ought to ensure that the arts do not transgress the bounds of social utility: "cette même politique doit en resserrer l'emploi dans les bornes indiquées par leur utilité même." The concrete proposals (regulation of taste, allowing artistic activity only by those who have been checked for propriety, judgment, and moral integrity) tend toward a flexible cultural politics.[21]

The very factors which contribute to art's dangerous character offer at the same time the means of its instrumentalization. Emotional impact, the primary purpose of the fine arts ("leur but immédiat est de nous toucher vivement [their primary purpose is to move us]") can be employed for a "higher purpose": to mediate the fundamental social values (*maximes fondamentales*). In this view, art solves a central problem of the Enlightenment: how insights rationally arrived at might penetrate the subject's behavioral disposition [*Verhaltensdisposition*] which is much more susceptible to emotional impulses than to rational ones. In other words, art solves the theory-practice problem. It is interesting to note that the author of the article also discusses the functional determination of art under the rubric of the stabilization of society. In times of crisis (*conjunctures critiques* or *moments de crise*) it is precisely the "fine arts" that help us to associate pleasure with the most dreary duties.[22]

While pressing art into immediate service for achieving moral-political goals, the article mentions a second functional determination. This could be called "humanizing":

The task of the fine arts, of our dwellings, gardens, furniture, and especially of our language, the most important of our inventions, is to ornament [*revêtir d'agréments*], not only, as some unjustly claim, to give us a merely outward pleasure in attendant attractions, but above all to give our minds and hearts a refined attitude and a nobler character by means of the gentle impression of what is beautiful, harmonious, and charming.

Two points should be emphasized here: first, the fact that a close connection between art and the everyday is clearly at issue. In no way is art juxtaposed with everyday life as a realm of higher ideals; it ought rather to be integrated in it. Beyond that, we can also detect the interests of the manufacturing and merchant bourgeoisie who make their living from the production of luxury goods. Second, we should note that the humanizing impact of artistic creations appears to obey certain aesthetic norms of harmony and appropriateness (*harmonieux et convenable*). At another point the concept of order is introduced as an aesthetic category. On the one hand, the Enlightenment-bourgeois institution of art draws strength from its rejection of a courtly (aristocratic) notion of art which reduces the function of art to pleasure (note the rejection of a *jouissance stérile et non réfléchie des attraits sensuels* [the sterile and unreflected rapture of sensual attraction]). On the other, the aesthetic norms of [French] classical courtly art were adopted by the Enlightenment-bourgeois institution of art, since only they can guarantee the end of humanization. It is here that the groundwork is laid for the canonization of the classical in advanced bourgeois society.[23]

Above all, the article "Beaux arts" advances a functional determination of art. It is exactly art's irrational character, which represents a potential danger to a social whole grounded on rationality, that becomes the point of departure for a conception that hopes to set up art as a means of humanizing and moral education of humanity. Because of the high level of generality of its problematic, the article does not pay attention to the fact that a particular *artistic material* and a particular *attitude of reception* accompany the institution of the concept of art. We will elaborate this argument in a brief examination of Diderot's *Eloge de Richardson*.[24]

In this essay, Diderot treats literature as a way of mediating moral-political insights and thus separates the sensuous concreteness of the novel's mode of representation from the abstractness of the moral maxim. Beyond that, the essay illuminates the relationship between a general notion of literature, artistic material, and attitude of reception, which the concept of the institution of art/literature encompasses as a whole. Diderot clarifies the changes in literary material in relation to Richardson's innovation. Instead of "illusory happenings" we have a plausible plot ("le monde où nous vivons est le lieu de la scène [the world in which we live is the site of the action]"); the characters portrayed there are taken from the social milieu ("ses caractères sont pris du milieu du societé"). The attitude of reception is determined through the recipient's identification with the morally positive hero[ine] and through her or his moral distaste for the less worthy. Diderot claims to have enriched his experience as a result of reading Richardson: "je sentais que j'avais acquis de l'expérience."

The analysis of the texts provides a complex and contradictory picture of the Enlightenment-bourgeois institutionalization of art. Formulations in which the autonomy of the realm of art is set up (such as in notions of its origin in spontaneous aesthetic praxis, natural beauty, impact on the senses) in particular suggest that the instrumentalization of art can *also* be understood as an attempt to associate an overwhelmingly irrational praxis with a form of social life grounded in rationality.

The Bourgeois-Autonomous Institution
of Art/Literature[25]

> The ruling idea of the useful has slowly but surely repressed that of the noble or the beautiful; we contemplate even great sublime Nature only with the eyes of financiers [*mit kameralistischen Augen*] and find the picture interesting only insofar as we can calculate the value of its products.
>
> In the establishment of rank and trade, the question is not whether this rank or that trade affects those who practice it, whether it weakens body and mind or keeps them healthy, whether it helps to direct Nature's ends to the edification of the human mind; rather, we always seem to regard a part of a human being as a mere tool in the hand of another who is in turn a tool in the hand of a third, and so on.[26]

When Goethe's friend, Karl Philipp Moritz, laments the damaging aloofness of the "well-bred part" of humanity from those who "build the earth by the sweat of their brow," he appears at first glance quite close to the Encyclopedists, who champion the revaluation of the mechanical arts.[27] What is at issue in both cases is the recognition of the working populace in society; Moritz, however, is not speaking of manufacturing workers or artisans, but of farmers. Yet Moritz does not ground the desired recognition of the working populace in their social utility but, rather, in that principle of utility which makes people into means rather than their own ends. Whereas the Encyclopedists treat the principle of utility as the highest value, Moritz regards it negatively.

For Moritz the counterprinciple to the "ruling idea of utility" is the idea of beauty, whose essential traits come from its opposition to utility: "We can therefore recognize the beautiful only insofar as we oppose it to the useful and separate the former as sharply as possible from the latter."[28] If the Encyclopedists had devalued the fine arts against the "useful and necessary liberal arts" and concerned themselves with instrumentalizing them, Moritz valued the very purposelessness of the work of art: "The purpose of the beautiful does not lie outside itself; it exists because of its own inner completeness, not because of the completeness of something else."[29] Implied here is a new institutionalization of art, which is radically other than the Enlightenment-bourgeois institution. Instead of an instrument of an external moral or philosophical end, the work of art is identified as its own end.

In the new institutionalization of art as autonomous, the classical aesthetic offers not only a general concept of art but also a new aesthetic norm and a new attitude of reception. The *aesthetic norm* is that of the organic whole whose parts have a functional relation to the whole: "By use, we understand the connection between a thing, considered as a part, and the cohesion of things which we think of as a whole. . . . From this we can see that, in order not to be useful, something has to be necessary to a whole that exists for its own sake, and that the concept of the beautiful must entail the concept of a whole that exists for its own sake."[30] The relationship between the establishment of art's autonomy and the model of the organic whole that functions as an aesthetic norm emerges here. Only the "whole existing for its own sake" can be considered purposeless. That the concept of the organic, living thing stands behind Moritz's concept of the whole is clear in his critique of allegory. So he finds fault with the allegorical figure of Justice, arguing that it is composed merely of the juxtaposition of diverse signs (scale, sword, blindfold): "Nothing is more contrary than this figure; nothing in it is active or in motion; it holds the sword and the scales in a merely mechanical fashion, and its blindfolded eyes only emphasize its inaction. The whole figure is overburdened and stands there like a dead mass, weighed down by itself."[31] What Moritz finds wanting in allegorical representation is above all the absence of movement; the figure is no living whole and therefore has no beauty.

The *attitude of reception* in the Enlightenment-bourgeois institution-alization of art is marked by the recipient's identification with the re-presented figure. The recipient enriches her or his experience through confronting his or her own experience with the work. The reception of autonomous works of art is conducted differently, according to Moritz:

> When the beautiful draws our attention entirely to itself, it takes our attention away from ourselves so that we appear to lose ourselves in the beautiful object [of our attention]; this very loss, this forgetting of ourselves is the highest degree of pure, disinterested delight that the beautiful gives us. In this moment we sacrifice our narrow, individual existence to a higher mode of being.[32]

In the act of reception, a radical separation from the experience of everyday life ("our narrow, individual existence") is achieved. Aesthetic reception, like a religious experience, is understood as a "higher mode of being." The recipient's interest is directed not so much toward the object of the repre-sentation as toward the form: "When we look at Guido's *Fortune*, we pay no attention to the vagaries of luck but rather take delight in the outline and the plenitude of this lightly and delicately executed form."[33]

A sociohistorical explanation of the aesthetic of autonomy, the first con-sistent formulation of which we owe to Moritz, still needs to be researched further, despite some significant attempts. It seems to me important to in-dicate the uneven breadth of these attempts. Robert Minder rightly points to the influence of Pietism on Moritz's aesthetic (particularly relevant in the erasure of the actual recipient in the act of reception).[34] We ought nonetheless to take into account that explanations of this kind, which are attached to the real social experiences of a particular author, despite their undeniable plausibility, do not fully allow for the institutionaliza-tion of the concept of autonomous art in advanced bourgeois society. In order to understand why the concept of autonomy was able to prevail— not without controversy—against the Enlightenment-bourgeois concept of art, we return to explanatory models that treat the functional mechanism of bourgeois-capitalist society as a whole.

This explanatory model must be so conceived that it renders compre-hensible both the genesis of the concept of autonomy in a particular period and its enduring validity. As I see it, there are two propositions that ful-fill this demand: explanation by way of market mechanisms or by way of the problematic of alienation. As Jochen Schulte-Sasse has shown, the establishment of literature as autonomous art in Germany is linked to the trivialization of the Enlightenment view of literature, which can be seen as a response to the expansion of the literary market at the end of the eighteenth century.[35] The exponential growth in book publication in Germany during the last third of the century makes trivial or mass-market literature a problem. *One* answer to that problem is what Schulte-Sasse calls the "esotericization" of literature: the withdrawal of the Enlightenment-bourgeois demand for engaged writing for all, and thus the return to an elite audience. This would explain literature's increasingly esoteric character but not the aesthetic of autonomy itself. Martin Fontius, who has offered the most systematic argument on this subject in recent years, attempts to explain the aesthetic of autonomy on the basis of the subordination of literature to the laws of the market. The fact, supported by evidence from sources, that writers at the turn of the century perceived "admiration" and "reward" as hindrances to the creation of a perfect work of art is interpreted by Fontius as evidence that artists have become aware of their new relationship to society as commodity producers.[36] The most impressive piece of evidence that Fontius presents comes from the late-Enlightenment writer Charles Garve, who notes: "Since the market price of every commodity is different from its inner worth, the former determined by competition and by the customers' demand, the latter by the time and effort expended on the work, relationships between writer and publisher emerge which are not to the writer's advantage."[37] There is thus no doubt that Garve grasped the changes underlying the literary work's transformation into a commodity: that is, the "division in the labor product" between use value (or "inner worth") and exchange value (or "market price") (Marx).

It is extremely signficant nonetheless that Garve, who had remarkable insight for his time into the contradictions affecting the commodity form of literature, does not quite conclude with an absolute opposition of "inner worth" and exchange value, as is (implicitly) the case with Moritz. Instead, Garve retains an Enlightenment view of literature and the notion of the "popular character of diction" [*Popularität des Vortrages*] as an evaluative criterion for the work.[38] Despite his awareness of the contradictory character of commodity form, Garve refuses to sacrifice one aspect of the work of art ("inner worth") to the other ("market price" or "popularity"); he is concerned rather with their mediation. Karl Philipp Moritz and the theorists of autonomy take another road: they hypostasize the "inner worth" of the work of art at the expense of its accessibility.

In my view, this is the point at which an explanation of the aesthetic of autonomy is no longer sufficient in itself. We have seen that Moritz sees the essence of the work of art in its purposelessness and that he determines the beautiful in opposition to the useful. The peculiar use value of the work is supposed to emerge only in the destruction of all purposeful determination. The opposition to the "ruling idea of utility" cannot be derived from the commodity form. At this point we have to turn to that problematic of alienation which Moritz himself addressed. A line of thought from the passage quoted at the beginning of this section might help us here: how can the human individual be maintained as totality in a society organized according to the division of labor? Moritz sees the problem of the separation of manual and intellectual labor and describes it as alienation. Manual laborers are forced to execute something which they themselves have not created. Social relations are what compel them.

> The cunning and crafty part of humanity has found means to deprive the Christian and well-meaning person of his fundamental needs in some way and to restore them only under the condition that he relinquish for a while the natural connections between forces of mind and body and, like a mere machine, stretch his arm according to the thought of another and lift his foot, just as the soldier must do on command.[39]

Whereas the Encyclopedists protest against the limited social recognition accorded manual labor, Moritz criticizes it as alienated labor, in the precise sense that it is determined not by itself but by an alien force. Moritz does not draw political conclusions from this critique, however, but only aesthetic ones.

A third explanatory proposition remains. That the aesthetic of autonomy acquired certain aspects of religious experience cannot be attributed to Karl Philipp Moritz's life alone: a crude opposition between the everyday world and art, a worshipful attitude toward the work of art, in short, those moments in the relation between work and recipient which Benjamin called "aura." This sort of reliance on religious models makes sense only in a period in which religious worldviews have begun to lose their obligatory character.

The explanatory propositions presented here should not be interpreted as "factors" in terms of a positivistic sociology of art but rather as moments of a historical process. The context can be easily noted at a high level of abstraction. A commodity-producing society presupposes a division of labor and with it a tendential alienation, just as the long-term "dissemination of the subsystems of conduct based on instrumental reason" casts doubt on the "legitimation of power based on cosmological worldviews."[40] The task of a sociology of art and literature investigating the transformation over time of art as an institution is to grasp this interconnectedness in a historically concrete fashion.

If we compare the notion of autonomous art in Moritz's formulation with the Enlightenment-bourgeois institution of art, we would have to note that, despite the differences which we have tried to demonstrate, a certain similarity emerges: humanization as a goal. "The nobility and refinement of the beautiful work of art depends on the degree to which the human mind can be ennobled and refined through contemplating that work."[41] As is well known, Schiller also finally attached an apparently purposeless art to a purpose, namely to the education of humanity. Insofar as this move attributes to autonomous art a moral-philosophical goal orientation, the representatives of autonomous art can always make their case with moral concepts.[42] That both sides of the autonomous concept of art (purpose-lessness and the purpose of humanization) could part ways in the course of the evolution of art in bourgeois society should not displace the unity of the bourgeois institution of art/literature. Its boundary is crossed only when the autonomous status of the work of art is challenged.

One more essential difference between the Enlightenment and autono-mous concepts of art in Moritz's version ought to be noted. As we have seen, the Enlightenment concept of art retains a moment that threatens the social order. This moment lies in art's capacity for arousing the irra-tional potential of human beings. The writer of the article on *beaux arts* took steps to prevent the liberation of this moment. In Moritz's aesthetic, such measures are no longer needed. Art understood as a "higher mode of being" no longer threatens to arouse unsatisfied desires. That aspect, omitted from the classical formulation of the aesthetic of autonomy, is nonetheless introduced into the concept of autonomy by the early Roman-tics; in this context, however, in contrast to the Enlightenment view of art, the irrationality of art is seen in a positive light: "For that is the beginning of all poetry, to transcend the laws and the process of right reason and to transport us once again to the beautiful confusion of the imagination, to the primal chaos of human nature, for which I as yet know no symbol more beautiful than that of the bright throng of the old gods."[43] Moritz criticized thinking in terms of means and ends and conceived of art as the social realm which is not subject to that sort of thinking. Friedrich Schlegel radicalizes this critique and opposes poetry absolutely to "right reason." Poetry ought to aid the emergence of those irrational forces which the Enlighteners tried to banish. That move affects the realm of aesthetic norms: instead of the organic totality of the artistic image, concepts like the return of mythology, the fragment, irony, emerge. The work of art is no longer an ordered alternative world but rather an otherworld torn to bits. Thus is the aesthetic of autonomy's other pole formulated.

This early Romantic opposition of poetry and reason becomes in Nietzsche's hands in the late nineteenth century a radical separation of art and science, or of the tragic and the theoretical worldview. To the degree that bourgeois society masters external nature with the help of science and technology without solving the problem of the emerging proletariat, art tends to create a merely abstract otherworld against the real one, which in turn becomes more dangerous as the [individual] subject, the bearer of this otherworld, no longer represents the principle of bourgeois universality.[44]

Looking back on this outline of the functional transformation of art in the context of the bourgeoisie's seizure of political power, we should clearly see that the proposed category—institution of art—should be understood as a hermeneutic rather than a historical category. The point of introducing this category is to make possible a critique of the evolution of art in bourgeois society. The Enlightenment-bourgeois institution of art/ literature tends to treat the psychic domain in technological terms. The historicophilosophical critique of instrumental reason, developed by Horkheimer and Adorno in *Dialectic of Enlightenment,* a critique which also directs inner human nature toward externally established purposes, can be applied here. In contrast, the doctrine of autonomy seems to preserve the freedom of a partial domain in society against the attack of an all-powerful instrumental reason. But this emancipation in outline remains either a mere thought, which leaves the real world intact (Moritz), or it runs the risk of regressing into myth (Friedrich Schlegel).

Notes

1. See Werner Krauss, "Literaturgeschichte als geschichtlicher Auftrag," in *Studien und Aufsätze* (Berlin/GDR; 1959), 19–71; Wolfgang Kayser, *Das sprachliche Kunstwerk* (Bern, 1948).

2. The work of Krauss's student, Erich Köhler, is an exception. See his programmatic essay, "Über die Möglichkeiten historisch-soziologischer Interpretation," in *Esprit und arkadische Freiheit* (Frankfurt, 1972), 2:83–103.

3. Kayser, *Das sprachliche Kunstwerk*, 18.

4. Hans Robert Jauss, *Literaturgeschichte als Provokation* (Frankfurt, 1970); in English, "Literary History as Challenge," in *Towards an Aesthetics of Reception*, trans. Timothy Bahti (Minneapolis: University of Minnesota Press, 1982).

5. "Confounding the work with its genesis, as though becoming were the masterkey of what has become, leads essentially to aesthetic scholarship's alienation from art" (T. W. Adorno, *Ästhetische Theorie* [Frankfurt, 1970], 267); "Once works of art are buried in the pantheon of canonical commodities [*Bildungsgüter*], their truth-value is damaged" (339).

6. In particular, Adorno's adoption of the functional determination of classical aesthetics: "to the degree that art allows for a social function, that function is its functionlessness" (*Ästhetische Theorie*, 336ff.).

7. Walter Benjamin, *Das Kunstwerk im Zeitalter seiner Technischer Reproduzierbarkeit* (Frankfurt, 1963), title essay.

8. See Peter Bürger, *Theorie der Avantgarde* (Frankfurt, 1973); *Theory of the Avant-garde*, trans. Michael Shaw (Minneapolis: University of Minnesota Press, 1984).

9. Antoine Adam, *Histoire de la littérature française au XVIIe siècle*, 5 vols. (Paris, 1949–56).

10. Roland Barthes, "Histoire ou littérature?" (1960), in *Sur Racine* (Paris, 1963); "History or Literature?" in *On Racine*, trans. Richard Howard (New York: Hill and Wang, 1964).

11. Ibid., 149; 154.

12. Ibid., 150; 156.

13. Ibid., 152; 157.

14. See Jürgen Habermas, "Erkenntnis und Interesse," *Technik und Wissenschaft als "Ideologie"* (Frankfurt, 1968); *Knowledge and Human Interest* (London, 1978).

15. See "The Institution of Art as a Category of the Sociology of Literature," in this volume, and P. Bürger, *Theory of the Avant-garde*.

16. On the problem of the connection between institution analysis and the interpretation of single works, see the essays by P. Bürger on La Fontaine and Stendhal in *Aktualität und Geschichtlichkeit: Studien zum gesellschaftlichen*

Funktionswandel der Literatur, ed. Peter Bürger (Frankfurt, 1977), 21–47, 105–59.

17. J. Le Rond d'Alembert, "Discours préliminaire," *Encyclopédie* (1751).

18. Immanuel Kant, *Kritik der Urteilskraft,* in *Werke,* ed. W. Weisehedel (Darmstadt, 1968), 8:406 (Sec.46).

19. "Beaux arts," in *L'Encyclopédie ou dictionnaire raisonné des sciences, des arts, et des métiers* (Geneva, 1778), 1:484–91.

20. The fact that "courtly" and "aristocratic" were not identical in seventeenth-century France need not concern us here; see F. Nies, *Gattungspoetik und Publikumsstruktur. Zur Geschichte der Sévignébriefe* (Munich, 1972), 8ff.

21. This initially surprising phenomenon can be explained in relation to Lothar Paul's interpretation of Plato's critique of poetry and rhetoric. Because poetry and discourse about it are not skills [*techné*], i.e., not employed according to rational rules that can be learned but, rather, attributable to the enthusiasms of the bards [*Rhapsoden*], they represent foreign bodies invading the rational order of the Greek polis, grounded on the principle of commodity exchange. See Lothar Paul, *Geschichte der Grammatik im Grundriss* (Weinheim, 1978), 545ff. If this interpretation is correct, then the Encyclopedists' support for a restrictive cultural politics can be explained in analogous terms. With the ascendancy of capitalist commodity production, the problem of attaching an irrational praxis to a rational social order reemerges.

22. That the instrumental concept of literature contains the program of manipulation alongside that of enlightenment is clear in Schiller's essay "Was kann eine stehende Bühne eigentlich wirken?" (What is the actual impact of a stable theatre?): "It is no less possible—according to the rulers and guardians of the state—to guide the opinions of the nation as to government and governed. In the theater, the law-giving power might speak to its subjects in strange symbols, answering their complaints even before they are uttered, and allay their doubts without seeming to" (Friedrich Schiller, *Sämtliche Werke,* ed. G. Fricke and H. G. Goepfert [Munich, 1967], 5:829).

23. On this point, see H. Thoma, "Literatur-Didaktik-Politik: Zur Rezeptionsgeschichte der französischen Klassik," in *Romanistik-Bildung und Ausbildung* (Munich, 1978), 1.

24. The following citations are taken from Denis Diderot, "Eloge de Richardson," *Oeuvres esthetiques,* ed. P. Vernière (Paris, 1959), 29ff.

25. On this section, see Christa Bürger, *Der Ursprung der bürgerlichen Institution Kunst im höfischen Weimar* (Frankfurt, 1977), chap. 5.

26. Karl Philipp Moritz, "Das Edelste in der Natur," in *Werke in zwei Bänden,* ed. J. Jahn (Berlin, 1973), 1:236.

27. Ibid., 235.

28. Moritz, "Über die bildende Nachahmung des Schönen" (1788), in *Werke* 1:263.

29. Moritz, "Über den Begriff des in sich selbst Vollendeten," in *Werke* 1:205.

30. Moritz, "Über die bildende Nachahmung des Schönen," 264.

31. Moritz, "Über die Allegorie," in *Werke* 1:303.

32. Moritz, "Über den Begriff des in sich selbst Vollendeten," 206.

33. Moritz, "Über die Allegorie," 303f.

34. Robert Minder, *Glaube, Skepsis und Rationalismus* (Frankfurt, 1974).

35. Jochen Schulte-Sasse, *Die Kritik an der Trivialliteratur seit der Aufklärung* (Munich, 1971).

36. Martin Fontius, "Produktivkraftentfaltung und Autonomie der Kunst . . . ," in *Literatur im Epochenumbruch. Funktion europäischer Literaturen im 18. und beginnenden 19. Jahrhundert,* ed. G. Klotz et al. (Berlin, 1977), 498.

37. Charles Garve, quoted in ibid., 499f.

38. See Charles Garve, "Von der Popularität des Vortrages," *Popularphilosophische Schriften,* ed. K. Wölftel (Stuttgart, 1974), 1039–66.

39. Moritz, "Einheit—Mehrheit—menschliche Kraft" (1786), in *Werke* 1:250.

40. Jürgen Habermas, *Technik und Wissenschaft als "Ideologie,"* 68. Hans Sanders has examined the significance of the erosion of traditional norms for the development of the institution of art/literature in the novel; see "Institution Kunst und Theorie des Romans" (Ph.D. diss., University of Bremen, 1977).

41. Moritz, "Das Edelste in der Natur," 234.

42. The proximity of moralizing criticism and the program of *l'art pour l'art* during the July Republic in France, for example, can be understood as a split between the affirmative and the critical sides of the autonomous institution of literature, in the attempt to establish a concept of literature in opposition to the representatives of "social art." See H. Stenzel, "Der historische Ort Baudelaires" (Manuscript).

43. Friedrich Schlegel, "Gespräch über die Poesie," in *Kritische Schriften,* ed. W. Rasch (Munich, 1964), 502.

44. See G. Sautermeier, "Nietzsches Geburt der Tragödie," *Hefte für kritische Literaturwissenschaft* (Frankfurt, 1979), 1.

Christa Bürger

4.

Human Misery or
Heaven on Earth?

The Novel Between
Enlightenment and
the Autonomy of Art

The Historicity of the Dichotomy Problem

In a recently published social history of German literature, the Enlightenment novel is judged in terms that differ only in the abstract from negative judgments common in nineteenth-century literary histories:

> On hand from the start, the triviality of narrative was disseminated to a diffuse, if still largely bourgeois, public through deliberately increased production of the novel as commodity. . . . Authors such as Wezel or Knigge used the new situation to survive by writing a great deal, if only for a limited time, as "free-lance writers."[1] They stuck to the . . . reproduction of established conventions and helped extend the domain of the trivial and easily consumed to new "factory-like" dimensions.[2]

This judgment measures the Enlightenment novel against the aesthetic of autonomy. From this perspective, a functional determination of literature that treats the individual work as an instrument of bourgeois norms and of its self-realization can be criticized for subjecting literature to extra-aesthetic ends.[3] The above quotation shows the dilemma of the division of labor between literary scholarship and research on mass-market literature [*Trivialliteraturforschung*]. Literary scholars tend to detach the Enlighten-

An earlier version of this study, "Das menschliche Elend oder Der Himmel auf Erden. Zur Dichotomisierung von hoher und niederer Literatur am Ende des 18. Jahrhunderts in Deutschland," appeared in *Sprachkunst* 9, no. 2 (1978): 203–19.

ment novel from literature, treating it as "nonart," that is, outside their field of study. Researchers of mass-market literature find it worthy of investigation insofar as it represents a "mirror of the times," a historical document.[4] Common to both of these partial disciplines is the tendency toward trivializing the Enlightenment novel, which takes for granted the very dichotomy between high and low literature which ought to be the object of consideration. The question of the institutionalization of literature within which the Enlightenment novel is produced and received cannot be posed within this narrow problematic.

In the sixties, Eva Becker criticized this kind of normative narrowing of the field of literature and problematized the traditional distinction between the serious or "art" novel and the mass-market novel in the context of the eighteenth century.[5] As important as Becker's revision of the judgment on the Enlightenment novel is, her approach is still positivist, since she makes no attempt to grasp her object of study from the perspective of the novel's current stage of evolution; that is, she does not try to find a point of view that would allow her to extract contemporary significance from this investigation of the Enlightenment novel. Hence the weakness of her argument, which elicits the revaluation of the genre not from its potential present-day currency but from the prevailing conceptions of literature in the period. The evaluative practice of contemporary literary journalism [*Literaturkritik*] (such as the influential *Allgemeine deutsche Bibliothek* of the Enlightener Nicolai) is treated as "datum," although it should be interpreted as a moment in a historical evolution. Indeed, the last third of the eighteenth century is determined by the confrontation and competition between the Enlightenment-bourgeois and the autonomous conceptions of literature. Literary scholarship grounded in institutional and sociological analysis would attempt to grasp the reviewing practice of a contemporary critic as part of this process of confrontation. Nicolai, for example, represents a particular but not completely compelling conception within the contemporary discussion about the sociomoral or aesthetic significance of the novel. In a significant departure from the conception of the autonomy of the work of art, as developed in classical Weimar and early Romantic circles, he upholds an Enlightenment-bourgeois conception of literature focused on effect [*wirkungsbezogenen*]. In so doing, he judges the novel production of the period less according to aesthetic criteria than according to the novel's significance in the life-praxis of the recipient.

That a functional transformation of literature is indeed at issue here can be shown in the example of the *Werther* debate; in retrospect a contemporary described this debate as the *expression* of historical disputes around the institution of literature. Contemporary critics saw *Werther* in normative terms rather than as an autonomous work of art:

> [*Werther*] appears seductively to introduce a new moral based on passion at the cost of the old one based on reason. Most serious and comic polemical and satirical commentary provoked by the novel focused on this characteristic rather than on its aesthetic value. But it was the public's fault, not the author's, if people took these free representations of the human heart for moral directives. Readers were not yet able to deal with pure aesthetic interest directed toward the lively representation rather than the consideration of moral ends.[6]

In the context of research investigating the functional transformation of literature, the problem of the dichotomy between high and low literature is historically primary. Peter Uwe Hohendahl and Jochen Schulte-Sasse have discussed this process of dichotomization in the context of the development of the literary market and the problematizing of the Enlightenment aesthetic of effect.[7] I would like to examine another aspect of this dichotomization. The dissociation of art and life-praxis institutionalized by the aesthetic of autonomy leads to the cultural elite's alienation from requirements of broader classes of readers, which are directed toward norms and values. This alienation carries with it the danger of a false sublation or cancellation of that dissociation, through the emergence of a commercialized mass-market literature based on the reconciliation to the existing order. Moreover, the normative aesthetic contained in the postulate of autonomy gains a decisive significance in the elaboration of a canon of bourgeois literature. In the light of an analysis of concrete historical documents, I would like to discuss the following:

1. The process by which part of bourgeois literature is marked off as trivial in the context of a dispute between two distinct conceptions of literature—enlightenment and autonomy—fighting to establish themselves. The battle against mass-market literature can therefore be understood as a battle against the Enlightenment.

2. Under pressure from the conception of the novel based on an aesthetic

of autonomy, the Enlightenment novel changed in the direction of an affirmative—in the negative sense—mass-market literature.

Carl von Carlsberg; or, On Human Misery

The first part of Salzmann's *Carlsberg*, published in 1783, according to contemporary judgment, introduced a new "trend-era" [*mode-Epoche*] to German literature, as suggested by the number of reviews, imitations, and counternovels.[8] Given that, as early as the end of the eighteenth century, the novel was so thoroughly forgotten that the name Salzmann is hardly mentioned in literary histories from that time to the present, the issue deserves a historical explanation.[9] Begun *before* the French Revolution, devalued as historically outdated by the turn of the century, *Carlsberg* points to a stage in the novel's evolution which can obviously be criticized from the standpoint of the aesthetic of antonomy. Salzmann's *Carlsberg* was conceived of as an epistolary novel, whose letters provide a flexible plot framework for the aristocratic protagonist's love affair with a bourgeois girl. Without any psychological confusion or dramatic complications that might be occasioned by external intrigues, the love story moves directly to the happy union of the lovers. The novel's interest clearly cannot lie in this love story but rather, as the *Hamburgischer unparteiischer Correspondent* emphasized, in the "many striking episodes" which the letter writers communicate to one another,[10] especially the hero and the educators to whom he owes his social and moral upbringing: a Colonel von Brav, the prototype of the enlightened landed nobility, and the military chaplain Wenzel, who represents the program of princely education. These episodes all follow a simple schema: while walking, traveling, or involved in daily affairs, during expedition or raids, the hero and his friends discover human misery, to which they react in two ways: they attempt to find out, by reasonable means—in conversation with the victims and the perpetrators—the grounds for this evident misery, and they try to offer aid in concrete individual cases.[11]

What Salzmann brings to light here is the following: the barbaric residue of feudal power; the legal practice of intolerant representatives of clerical institutions still trapped in the Middle Ages, which still profoundly affects human relations; jurisprudence, not yet humanized by the notions of equality characteristic of a developing bourgeois society, which functions as torture preceding execution; the barbarity of soldiers' lives (such as running the gauntlet); the pitiful condition of education, especially in rural areas; the health-endangering ignorance of a medical profession still upholding superstitious practices; the crudity of academic custom and the narrow-mindedness of ignorant professors; the organization of common institutions (such as orphanages) for the purposes of exploitation; and also the suffering that can be traced to capitalist modes of production that are gradually establishing themselves (such as the suffering of those working at home for textile distributors).[12]

In Salzmann's novel, the process of education is not represented through the peculiar subjectivity of a chosen individual; the individual is there only as a formal link between individual episodes. The only important thing for him is the subject matter, social reality, "human misery," which is exactly what the elevation of the novel to the status of a work of art impedes, in the view of the autonomy aesthetic of Weimar classicism. In this context, the social reality of human misery is not shattered or ameliorated by a subject appropriating and reworking that reality but appears rather as raw matter in all its artless clarity. What Salzmann portrays is nothing other than the reader's everyday experience, otherwise repressed or blunted by habit, which he compels to sustain a confrontation with reality. The shock, which mere looking should unleash in anyone witnessing misery, and which the reading of the novel should provoke because of Salzmann's refusal to rework reality in any artistic fashion, is addressed on occasion by the witness, Carlsberg, who warns his reader: "Prepare yourself to read one of the worst scenes which ever existed on God's earth."[13] The terror of the realistic scene provokes the need in the protagonist for an understanding of the means by which society produces misery. Following each scene is a dialogue that is intended to clarify the cause of this misery; this is in turn succeeded by interventional action. Although dissociated in later institutionalization of literature, art, and life-praxis, social action and artistic activity form a unity for Salzmann.[14]

Carlsberg was written and received within an Enlightenment-bourgeois institution of literature. Salzmann's didactic-aesthetic program, which heralds the English social novel,[15] treats the novel as a suitable means of propagating Enlightenment norms and values in the life-praxis of those classes who cannot as yet participate in the "philosophical" discussion, or the elaboration of normative concepts, because of their lack of education. Within the bounds of this concept of literature, the individual work is judged according to the social effect for which it is striving; the question in this case is whether the artistic means employed here are the right ones to achieve the desired effect. Campe, for example, in the *Vorrede* [preface] to his adaption of *Robinson Crusoe*, requires that books lead "not merely to passive contemplation or to leisurely pathos, but immediately to *spontaneous activity [Selbsttätigkeit]*";[16] Johann Carl Wezel maintains that only a book that is "created out of our present-day world" suits the "goal of affecting a significant part of the community through useful industry in so far as that is possible in our world and according to our constitution."[17] And Salzmann, who offers an enthusiastic picture of the affective and effective possibilities [*Wirkungsmöglichkeiten*] of the writer in the *Beylage* [supplement] to the fifth part of his novel, stresses that his intention is not to create an aesthetically perfect work of art but rather an object for use.[18] He thus deliberately chooses his material to serve his pedagogic purposes. Salzmann would like his novel to persuade his readers, by way of a "true picture of present-day conditions," that "their misery is really still very great"; "I shall wrap [this portrayal] in a novelistic garment . . . to give it greater access to diverse classes of readers."[19]

But the Enlightenment project oversees not only the choice of material (or genre) but also the techniques of representation. Salzmann would like to speak "like the people" [*in Volkston reden*]; as G. Häntzschel has shown, he makes use of those literary models that were familiar to the lower, or popular, classes—chapbooks, almanacs, songbooks, and catechisms. Salzmann thus realizes a demand raised by Merck, who argues that the atrophy of the bourgeois intelligentsia's experience resulted in the absence of the realistic novel in Germany. He expects authors to renew the material and to make the "naiveté of the ordinary man, the person whose experience is really physical," the yardstick of their narration in a way that is focused on concrete particulars and an unalienated mode of perception.[20] Even at the end of the 1770s, Merck continued to uphold the literary conceptions of Sturm und Drang, which had its moment of truth, despite the movement's irrationality, in its opposition to the tendencies of the period and in its attempt to think through the possibility of the unification of bourgeois Enlightenment and popular literature. To be sure, Salzmann is not concerned to resuscitate a popular literature that has already been repressed by a developing modern society, nor to rearticulate its archaic-anarchistic urge toward freedom. His conception of literature is rather part of that rationalistically bounded bourgeois culture against which Sturm und Drang rebelled. We must also acknowledge that Salzmann also pushed the evolution of the novel significantly in the direction of montage and documentary, narrative forms which would once again be given up under pressure from the aesthetic of autonomy and the normative authority granted to the organic work of art.[21] Only in our century, in the context of the historical avant-garde movements, do the effective and affective possibilities of montage and documentary manifest themselves fully.[22] The historical place of the criterion of triviality or marketability is here: it informs the possibility of playing off fiction against documentary and of devaluating the novel that has social effectiveness as its goal against the works of autonomous art.

The Novel between Enlightenment and Autonomy

The assimilation of *Carlsberg* by contemporary criticism suggests that *diverse* conceptions of literature coexisted *side by side* during this period. From an Enlightenment-bourgeois standpoint, the novel's form is not problematic.[23] But even J. C. Wezel, himself an author of an Enlightenment novel, is visibly concerned to unify the influence of engagement and "the concept of a beautiful work of art," which he sees as a "poetic whole."[24] Aesthetic criticism of *Carlsberg* targets above all the absence of plot unity in the novel and the figure of the hero. In an anonymous contribution, *Über den dramatischen Roman* in 1791, the author single-mindedly represents the perspective of the 1790s, already influenced by the aesthetic of autonomy as propagated by certain writers' circles, in that he starts with the premise that "every work of art should be a harmonious whole"; Salzmann's name is not mentioned, but this criticism is aimed precisely at the novelistic form he practiced, namely, the "dialoguized novel."[25] The critics presume the consensus of contemporary literary connoisseurs on the definition of novels as only those works "that envisage the representation of character."[26] This definition has consequences for plot construction: "For those who give it some thought, the novel is a chain of incidents that are most intimately connected, a chain of causes and effects, which result in the solution of a psychological problem."[27] Hence the demand that the characters of a novel must be seen to act if the reader is to take an interest in them.[28] The writer criticizes the "dramatic" novel for going against this rule; the characters do not act, they merely feel, judge, rationalize;[29] in other words, they do not engage the reader's imagination.

The contemporary criticism summarized here is only seemingly confined to the *form* of *Carlsberg*; it focuses equally on the novel's intended effect.[30] Linked to the demand for plot construction that would present the hero's character as the result of a process of education is the dismissal of the partisan novel, the documentary novel, which is designed to communicate particular value conceptions and experiences of reality.[31] The anonymous critic rejects the type of work "in which the truth is already given, the plot already in place, and the character already determined."[32] Implied here is a tradition which is still effective today: criticism adopts the task of excluding certain texts as "nonart" and of trivializing those literary works which thematize social problems. The criterion for this discrimination is the indivisibility of "art" and "tendency."[33]

Criticism such as this, which would deny artistic character to a novel focused on the effect of its social critical content, applies criteria that are lacking from the beginning in Salzmann's novel, for this novel is produced and received within an Enlightenment-bourgeois institutionalization of literature. Within the bounds of the conception of autonomy, categories such as that of the organic work cannot lay claim to validity.

Contemporary claims that *Carlsberg* is lacking in reality are conducted rather differently. This claim, which challenges the accuracy of the actual experience that Salzmann presents, raises the question of realistic presentation, but within the bounds of Enlightenment-bourgeois conceptions of literature. Salzmann must defend himself against this criticism, which he does in the second printing of the book.: "My book has often been censured. . . . The limitless diversity of human opinions can only mean that a writer who does not agree with the tone of his contemporaries, but rather describes everything as he feels it, cannot but displease many people. Perhaps this displeasure is itself proof that he has indeed *seen with his own eyes*."[34] Salzmann revalues the censure of contemporary criticism as a sign that the readers take his knowledge and experience of reality seriously as a contribution to the contemporary debate about norms pertaining to social relations.[35]

If Salzmann pays any attention at all to justifying the representation of misery, it is when he has one of his figures reflect on the differing judgments of realistic representation by contemporary criticism. He has an enlightened lady of the court respond to her sister's letter, which had contained a report of a murder committed by her chambermaid, who had been seduced by the sister's husband:

To spare you any accusations, I would very much wish that your letter did not circulate in public. You might have been able to depict in the most vivid way the first meeting between your husband and the unfortunate woman and you would have rightly found many readers of both sexes. But to speak of the horrible consequences of the act, the blood, the trembling of limbs, twinges of conscience—that offends good taste, that is too crude.[36]

Here Salzmann criticizes contemporary reviewing practice; in this respect, his arguments correspond to those of conservative critics.[37] He attacks the immoral influence of romances.[38] It is more significant, it seems to me, that the contemporary critics take Salzmann's realism to task for "exaggeration."[39]

The sharpest attack on Salzmann's novel came from Karl Phillipp Moritz in a short essay, "Das menschliche Elend," published in 1786, at a time when Moritz had already developed his theory of the autonomy of the artwork, at least in essay form. Nonetheless, his contribution to the *Carlsberg* debate focuses exclusively on content, which is all the more surprising, in light of the frequent use by other critics of criteria such as organicity, unity, and so on, in determining a work's aesthetic quality. Moritz's procedure needs historical clarification. We ought to note on the one hand that the validity of the Enlightenment-bourgeois concept of literature was still more or less undisputed during the 1780s. On the other, the emphasis on content in Moritz's critique itself confirms my thesis that the battle against mass-market literature is also a battle against the Enlightenment's social critique. This fight was fought on two fronts: (1) general notions about literature—the demand for the autonomy of the work of art and the exclusion of an (instrumental) literature directed toward social effect—and (2) content—in this case, the "objectivity" of an autonomous (or conformist) literature is pitched against a critical representation of reality.

This is Moritz's point; he criticized *Carlsberg* for the Enlightenment program contained in the novel. He attempts to sublate the concept of misery—whose actuality he cannot deny—into the realm of philosophical reflection. In his view, human misery is the result of self-interest; Moritz, like Salzmann, conceives of self-interest in materialistic terms, as a characteristic of a (capitalist) society organized according to economic principles, in particular, that of private property, and thus sees the "general source of human misery" in class antagonism. This antagonism cannot be "blocked," since "so long as there are *oppressors*, there will also be *the oppressed*."[40] On the basis of the experience that "it would be unbearable for me to live in a world in which any thinking and feeling being was *necessarily* really unhappy," Moritz then attempts to argue away the idea, using the activity of the imagination, historical-philosophical speculation, and art.[41]

Human misery, or so he argues, is merely a product of the imagination,[42] and can be conceived of only as the "misery of the individual human being, not as that of humanity as a whole." "When misery is thus *individualized*, its imaginary weight falls away, and almost completely disappears if you consider *this individuation over time*; it is only the *present moment* in which the *individual human being really* bears the weight of misery; the individual does not possess *any sum* of misery."[43] The historical-philosophical speculation according to which history is understood as the process of humanity's gradual perfection grasps this process in a dialectical manner. Like Schiller and Kant, Moritz treats contradictions in society as the necessary condition of process; from this perspective, "self-interest" appears to be a productive force.[44]

Most significant for the evolution of literature is Moritz's aesthetic theory developed on the basis of his reflections on society; the social function of this theory lies precisely in the dispute with the Enlightenment novel. The experience of suffering spurs Moritz to theoretical exertion; his answer to it is, however, fundamentally different from Salzmann's. Moritz represses the unbearable idea of necessary misery in

> the consoling idea, tested by experience, that human beings are capable
> . . . [at every moment of their existence] of withdrawing into them-
> selves and freely abandoning everything around them to chance. . . .
> Only from within this secure fortress do I feel strong enough to rep-
> resent that which oppresses and torments human beings as an *object
> of my cold-blooded contemplation*, because I am composed no matter
> whether these people are helped or not. And so I let human misery in
> its terrible shapes *pass by my soul* and *reflect* on how all that evolves
> on the kind of straw that has sprouted from this decomposing seed,
> and on how dungeon and fortress, sword and wheel, monasteries
> and madhouses, war and plague, all these monstrous disharmonies,
> are *once again dissolved in general harmony*. . . . Should these *sweet*

thoughts be only a dream, I will still not waver—for I have learned *to withdraw into the moment of my being*, when everything around me falters. (Emphasis added)[45]

By means of human imaginative power manifested in the work of art, which is able to transcend reality, and by means of the transfiguring appearance of the beautiful, the painful process of history, in which destruction and development are necessarily interconnected, is dissolved into the suffering of individuals. The passage cited here sounds like a retort to Salzmann's remark in an attempt to persuade his readers "that, despite all the Enlightenment in our century, there is still an indescribable amount of misery and lamentation on our planet," and especially that all misery is socially produced and is not immutable. As soon as human understanding is "completely convinced that certain evils can be got rid of, the possibility of doing so is already there."[46] On the basis of this conviction, Salzmann contests precisely the contemplative consideration of misery that Moritz attempted. "Error" is the term he uses to describe the attitude of a man who "[sits] on his sofa, soaking his tart in burgundy, believing that, because he is comfortable, every living thing should also be, and that wisdom shines from every human institution, every folly can be explained away as guiltless and the necessary consequences of culture."[47] Salzmann's view, which keeps the individual detail in sight and treats the general progress of culture as dependent on particular improvements that must be concretely achieved, is opposed to the demand for *ideality* placed on the work of art. Wilhelm von Humboldt's formulation of this idea is the most radical: "to transform this enormous mass of singular and isolated appearances into an undivided unity and an organized whole." "To banish accident," is also Salzmann's goal for his literary efforts, but he does not try to achieve this goal by advancing on the road toward the dissociation of art and life-praxis but, rather, by producing an art understood as a form of social praxis.[48]

This juxtaposition should show that Moritz and Salzmann take as their points of departure two radically distinct and unreconciled views of art: Moritz's critique of Salzmann on the basis of an aesthetic theory grounded in the radical dissociation of art and life-praxis is also a way of settling accounts with the aesthetic of the Enlightenment, or with its evaluation of literature according to its interventional character and its significance for the life-praxis of the recipient.

One further aspect of the dispute between Salzmann and Moritz that seems important to me is its engagement with the problematic of *affirmation,* which has often been used in the delineation of boundaries between serious literature and entertainment since the reception of Critical Theory [of the Frankfurt School] by West German literary scholars. In his ground-breaking essay "On the Affirmative Character of Culture," which builds on the ideology critique of the early Marx, Herbert Marcuse shows that culture in bourgeois society admits human values only in the form of fiction and thus prevents their realization in the world. At the same time, Marcuse insists on treating this concept of culture dialectically and thus stresses the critical moment of art, which he understands as a protest against the bad constitution of society. "To be sure, [affirmative culture] exonerated 'external conditions' from responsibility for 'determining the lives of human beings [*Bestimmung des Menschen*],' thus stabilizing the injustice of those conditions. But it also held up to them as a task the image of a better order." [49] It is certainly true that present-day mass-market literature no longer permits this dialectic determination; it not only conceals contradictions in society but also relinquishes the counterimage which serious art, in Marcuse's view, held up to reality. We should consider the fact that, despite Salzmann's explicitly conservative attitudes,[50] opponents of the Enlightenment nonetheless feared that his social criticism, focused as it was on reforms, would undermine the foundations of feudalism's legitimacy,[51] and also the fact that Moritz's aesthetic theory, which can be linked to the historical experience of alienation encouraged by increasing division of labor, points clearly to moments in which the bad status quo is illuminated.[52] In so doing, we would have to admit that the question as to whether the Enlightenment-bourgeois *or* the autonomous conception of literature should be seen as affirmative was posed wrongly.[53] The ideas about literature of those two authors, here representing competing institutionalizations of literature at the end of the eighteenth century, are marked by both positions, which can be traced back to the social contradictions of the period in which these ideas emerged. If the problematic of the doctrine of autonomy as propagated by Moritz lies in the *harmonizing* tendency, which in turn corresponds to a contemplative (resigned) attitude of reception, then the danger of the Enlightenment-bourgeois institutionalization of literature represented by Salzmann lies in its being reduced to a merely *instrumental understanding of literature* which in turn would reduce the recipient to a mere object of the effect that the literary producer wants to achieve.

The Debate about Popular Literature [Volksliteratur]

The writers of the period under discussion were well aware of the problematic of popular or folk literature [*Volksliteratur*]; it played a role in the dispute over judging popular romances [*Volksschriften*] or their authors. Studying the contemporary documents in this case, one comes up against a paradox: one might expect that the opposition between the Enlightenment-bourgeois and autonomous conceptions of literature would be set out in terms of aesthetic valuation, in which Enlightenment aesthetics would offer a positive evaluation of popular romances and the aesthetics of autonomy would reject them. This is not the case, however. The paradox is resolved as soon as one examines it in terms of content: the Enlightenment-bourgeois perspective criticizes the type of popular writer who writes with the intention of furthering social integration and thus who instrumentalizes literature in the direction of social conformity; the elite-autonomous position, on the other hand, allows for the endorsement of this functional determination of literature for the mass of readers.

Let us look more closely at the documents. Contributions to periodicals, especially magazines representing an Enlightenment concept of literature, tend as expected to offer an unconditional endorsement of a certain kind of novel identified as a popular romance. Moreover, a particular kind of argument tends to repeat itself: popular romances are treated as an exceptional category, in that they "represent a midway point between novel and moral lesson." [54] Once one abandons aesthetic criticism at the outset, one is able to emphasize the Enlightenment or moral function of these novels. The *Teutsche Merkur* and especially the *Kaiserlich-privilegierten Reichsanzeiger* represented this position and took up the task of presenting the work of "deserving popular writers." [55]

Since religious worldviews were gradually losing their normative function, thanks to the process of secularization reaching even the lowest classes, it became increasingly necessary to provide them with literature that might satisfy the growing need for orientation guides in an ever more opaque social reality. [56] This development can be seen in the many suggestions for founding "patriotic" societies, which were to solicit the help of philanthropic and enlightened citizens to organize the production and distribution of "good" literature with the goal of enlightening those social classes whose material circumstances made it impossible for them to buy books. [C. M.] Wieland's *Teutsche Merkur* described reading as a "need . . . that can without further ado be classed as nourishment." Hence all "true patriots," but especially the "authorities" (for Wieland, a positively viewed enlightened despotism), had a duty "to use all means available to distribute books at the lowest price, below even the tax on meat or bread."[57]

The understanding of literature expressed in the *Merkur* contains criteria of evaluation that support not the aesthetic perfection of the individual work but the work's potential for giving "practical advice" for "common life."[58] This perspective ought to place those authors who wrote instructional texts and attempted to achieve a "popular discourse" in first place in the "pecking order" of various classes of writers, ahead of those producing autonomous works. As Knigge writes: "We can therefore judge the *degree of a book's value* according to the effects that it has . . . . I would thus give primary place to those writers who improve and teach their readers in a practical way, next would be those who open bold new prospects in the speculative sciences, and lastly those who write merely to entertain."[59] The criterion which Knigge applies in his judgment of literary works is clearly that of social utility; in this regard, contribution to the development of bourgeois norms takes precedence even over scientific discovery.

Then there is a series of socially engaged late Enlightenment writers who find the development of a "folk" literature and thus also the disconnecting of serious and mass-market literature, of autonomous works of art for an elite readership and useful (in terms of bourgeois morality) romances for the lower classes, problematic. Referring for comparison to Greek literature as an expression of the democracy of the polis, Friedrich Bouterwek condemns the evolution of German literature under the aegis of learned men (or practical philosophy), for

> the good that the public gets from this is usually nothing more than the chaff that is now chopped up in popular romances, moral primers, school books, and so-called readers for common use, after the corn has been thrashed out. . . . If Greek literature in the time of Aristotle did not much influence the masses of the Greek nation through *popular fiction* then the lively communication of concepts in the reciprocal

engagement of the various social ranks was perhaps more useful than an entire library of popular romances would have been.[60]

Bouterwek, who defends even writers like Iffland or Gottfried August Bürger, that is, authors whose writing is intended to have a practical influence on life, against the charge of triviality, in this context nonetheless vehemently attacks an instrumentalization of literature which leads to the dissociation of "high and low virtue."[61] Contemporary fears become clear when we remember that positive reviews of those novels which the critics treated as popular fiction emphasized that these ought to contain "moral lessons" that were "completely appropriate for the horizons of the rank for which the book was intended."[62] In this perspective, Gellert becomes "healthy nourishment" "for the average man interested in improving himself."[63] In other words, literary works in this context were judged exclusively according to their function in social integration. This tendency was so compelling that some novelists themselves prepared moral lessons for their readers in the form of aphorisms. In a positive assessment of one such folk novel in the *Hamburgischer unparteiischer Correspondent*, for example, Knigge writes:

> The chapbook itself contains Klausen's poems and an extract from aphorisms collected by him under certain titles: books, reading, truth, wisdom, virtue, etc. . . . They are equally pithy and instructive. The content of the book thus fully corresponds to its title: moralbook [*Sittenbuch*] for good people of all classes, including middle and lower popular classes. It is a very useful book for our elementary schools, offering its teachers a plethora of material for the entertainment and moral education of their charges.[64]

One should see here that the doctrine of autonomy and certain elite tendencies among the Romantics were reactions on this instrumentalization of literature, the other side of the Enlightenment-bourgeois institution of literature. August Wilhelm Schlegel is right when he defends the old chapbooks against the Enlighteners and the notion, which emerges in Voss's translation of Virgil, that Virgil might be useful in the progress of agricultural technology.[65] Departing from his usual conception of literature in this context, Schlegel validates precisely the moment of tradition, the appeal of repetition, as against the historical evolution of a literary market, a process which gradually gives literature the form of a commodity and generates the (false) need for novelty.

> The elevated educated ranks of our nation have no literature, but the people, the common man, do. This literature consists of the countless chapbooks bearing the rubric "printed this year" which invite the naive belief that they will never be outdated and so they never are. Sometimes the people are misled by the attraction of novelty, but in general they remain true to their tastes and buy books that have been read for centuries, despite the enlighteners efforts to trick them out of these books and to substitute their wretched things. And so the people prove that they have imagination and feeling.[66]

Measured against a merely instrumental literature produced especially for the masses of readers in the peasant and proletarian underclass, the old chapbooks contain a subversive moment despite their intrinsically escapist character. Schlegel takes a concretely grounded position to the contemporary debate about the reading needs of new reading classes when he rejects the manipulative strategy that bypasses the well-read chapbooks because they allegedly "spoil" the "ideas" of the "common man" and substitutes new versions in which the subversive moment has been erased. An anonymous contributor to the *Berlinische Monatsschrift* describes this strategy thus:

> Since . . . the people are unwilling to be parted from some of the old books, we cannot merely introduce new ones but should rather improve the old ones covertly and gradually. We should especially remember that those who tie their shoes with bast want to be able to amuse themselves as well as the wealthy lord for whom they toil. Hence we should preach and moralize in moderation and, instead of trying to persuade them that they are not miserable, allow them to laugh a little and to forget their misery. This does not mean that I do not want to hear of preaching or morality. . . . Only we should not make the moral lesson too obvious; for then the peasant might as well point us to his sermonbook and read us only as a good work.[67]

This kind of document concretizes the danger of the instrumentalization of literature, which turns the recipient into an object of the socially integrative intentions of the producer.

The progressive attitude that appears to be articulated in Schlegel's defense of the chapbooks is, however, immediately retracted; the conclusions that the Romantics draw from their insight into the manipulative character of "popular romances" which abuse their readers in the name of enlightenment are not suitable for foregrounding the institution of literature from the sketched dilemma between enlightenment and autonomy.[68] On the contrary, their own production and reviewing activity furthers the dichotomization of literature. Friedrich Schlegel was dissatisfied with his brother's positive view of Gottfried August Bürger, who was attacked by Schiller for his efforts in the area of "national-popular poetry." He insists on a dichotomized concept of literature, whereas August Wilhelm's review offers a generous consideration of texts in which "independent art is unified with the dependence on the noble aim of education and admonition.[69] In November 1791, Friedrich Schlegel writes to his brother:

Since seeing you, I have thought a great deal about the art of poetry. I think that only a few words can be said in favor of the yardstick of influence on the *people* and thus the degree of pleasure and recreation they might gain from *public* poetry [*öffentliche Dichtkunst*]. Influence and happiness and the means to those ends cannot, however, be measured. This is the case for the *secret* as well as public art of poetry. The more intimately this *secret* art is tied to the characteristics of the few, of and for whom it exists, the more it fulfills its goal and so becomes perhaps inaccessible to the people. To be sure, these secrets are often sold for a word of praise, but I for my part would never display my innermost self as a freak of nature in a curiosity cabinet. If I were to take influence on the people as my point of departure, I would wish that the poet would completely penetrate the interests of those whom he would influence so as to investigate all their relationships.[70]

Here Friedrich Schlegel distinguishes literature produced for the entertainment of broad (popular) readership and calculated to achieve an effect of "happiness" and success from an esoteric literature.[71] He examines the first in terms of interest and attributes to it the representation of (real) relations; for him, the object of the popular novel is everyday life and the life world of the reader to whom the text is directed.[72] The "secret art of poetry" is explicitly defined as poetry for a "few"; its object is the (problematic) subjectivity of fictional figures in whom the select group of specialists in art, for whom they are intended, can recognize themselves. Here we return to a motif that was mentioned earlier: the dichotomy of serious and entertainment literature is articulated in terms of an opposition between subjectivity and everyday reality.

But insofar as serious (autonomous) literature abandons the task of representing the social problems of the time, it alienates itself from the ever-broader classes of bourgeois readers for whom the problems of inwardness, the preoccupation of authors of "art novels," are incomprehensible. This development is reflected in a review of a *Lesebuch für den Mittelstand* [Reader for the middle class] in the *Oberdeutsche allgemeine Literaturzeitung*. The reviewer succeeds in offering a precise and overarching definition of the middle class's attitude toward aesthetic phenomena. Following the remarks of Christian Garve, as expressed in his essay "Über Moden [On fashions]," [73] the author describes a specifically middle-class mode of reception:

Just as in clothing, way of life, and even in eating and drinking, the middle class can be distinguished by its solidity and robustness from the fashions, manners, and the glittering extravagance and luxury of the so-called great or noble world, so also in taste for science and art. Conditioning has habituated its members to seek the useful in any pleasurable object. They are used to regular diligence and uninterrupted work; pleasure is not their business, but rather brief recreation from business; not much variation is needed to make their short moments of pleasure palatable; they look more at the subject matter than at the form and cannot understand that a delicately made Grecian urn made of gypsum might be better than a badly made silver container, or that a fool might be worthy of life because he is well-bred. The same is true of their reading habits. They do not read merely to amuse themselves; rather they want to be instructed by every book they pick up during their leisure hours. The artistic novel is lost on them, because it does not clearly and definitely follow a moral truth or contain a true story. If they are not persuaded by the artistic novel, it is because they find the character's speech and behavior overwrought and unnatural, or because their own activities leave them little time for the study of human character, or because the range of their experience is too limited. Hence, apart from the Bible, only history books and travel accounts and at most a very proper moral novel are to be found on the bookshelf of a hardworking artisan (if indeed he has any desire at all for self-instruction and pleasure in reading).[74]

The citation clearly shows (and the critics are unanimous on this point) that the majority of bourgeois readers—insofar as they had any access to literary production—upheld an Enlightenment-bourgeois institutionalization of literature, from which they demanded not distraction or escape from the alienation of their professional and domestic daily lives but practical orientation, instruction, information. The direction of these legitimate requirements remains open: literature can lend itself equally to a critical, an emancipatory, or a socially integrative application.

From the Enlightenment Novel to Mass-Market Literature

We have seen how critics oriented toward the doctrine of autonomy reacted to the new needs of the reading public; their hostility toward the public offers no historically adequate solution to the problems outlined here. The question is how Enlightenment-bourgeois writers adopted and manipulated the new practical demands on literature. Salzmann's reaction to the critical reception of his *Carlsberg* may enable us to delineate a possible answer to the problem.

In the *Kaiserlich-privilegierter Reichsanzeiger* of 1796, Salzmann announced his new novel, *Der Himmel auf Erden*, in which he justified his departure from the material developed in *Carlsberg*. This announcement implies a break in the history of the Enlightenment-bourgeois novel, or writing for the people [Volksschrifttum], and the beginning of the evolution of the mass-market novel, an evolution that would cut short the novel's critical moment and lead eventually—and consequently—to the elaboration of the phenomena that Critical Theory subsumes under the concept of the consciousness industry. Salzmann writes:

> I wrote a book on human suffering . . . , since it was still a time when everyone could freely and openly express his opinion on anything. Now that night has fallen and, in a certain sense, nobody can effect anything, writing *Carl von Carlsberg* might well be no longer permissible. . . . Instead of the promised *Ludwig von Carlsberg* (in which I had planned to comment on certain pressing deficiencies in our civic constitution with as much zeal as in *Carlsberg*), I am now working on another book which leaves all forms of government unexamined and contains nothing but means by which everyone can be released from

human suffering and transform the world into heaven. To eliminate any suspicion of illusion, I ask the reader to ponder the following: that one can embellish a place remarkably if one changes the medium through which and the position from which one sees this place. . . . My purpose in writing this book is to accustom people to looking at the world in such a way that it seems like heaven to them. . . . It is my firm conviction today that everyone can find heaven anywhere, once he is persuaded by the fundamental principles that I will present in this book, and once he becomes used to judging and acting according to these principles. . . . [*Der Himmel auf Erden*] is intended above all for the educated classes, because I believe that they need it most. The more educated we are, the more deeply we feel any irregularities, the more manifold is our suffering. A play that is received with loud laughter by the uneducated often provokes loathing and resistance in the educated. Furthermore, the principles by which the latter class attempts to alleviate its slightest suffering no longer affect us, because we usually no longer believe in them. Nonetheless, I continue to write in such a way that even the lowest class understands me; in that way, I believe that my work will be useful to all.[75]

Salzmann grounds his proposed change of theme in social development: written before the French Revolution, his *Carlsberg* appeared during a period of relative press freedom. The last decade of the eighteenth century on the other hand is characterized by more stringent censorship measures, most clearly expressed by the attack on readers' societies, especially in the southern provinces of the German regime.[76] Salzmann uses a particular image: the night of limited freedom of opinion following the enlightened day.

The regressive social developments which he observes gives the Enlightener Salzmann an occasion to reconsider his own position; the result of this reflection is nonetheless not, as expected, a struggle against reaction by the writer engaged in social criticism but, rather—accommodation. Salzmann loses the reforming impulse of his early novel; he abandons the conception of literature informing *Carlsberg*, which treats the work as an active part of social practice. He no longer wants to change reality—even in terms of reform, within the parameters of an enlightened absolutism—but only people. More precisely, he wants to lead his readers to the point at which they absorb the "right" perspective and they see actuality with "new" eyes. When Salzmann spells out the purpose of his new book, it sounds like a precise response to the criticism of Karl Philipp Moritz: this book ought to show how the individual "can personally be released from human suffering." Moritz had found in the "comforting thought" "that it is within human power freely to submit oneself to necessity," a point of view from which the "monstrous dissonances" of the actual world could be dissolved into a "general harmony." In this schema, art explicitly becomes a new paradigm of reconciliation; since actual life is experienced as unchangeable, the subject ought to be persuaded that she or he can live within it. At issue, in other words, is the construction of a conformist consciousness.[77]

It is interesting to observe that Salzmann, who in *Carlsberg* had quite clearly represented himself as the advocate of the oppressed, no longer addresses lower-class readers but, rather, envisages recipients for the new novel as members of the "educated classes." Salzmann's self-representation offers a significant exemplum for the evolution of bourgeois culture. At this moment, material conditions of existence are no longer seen as the ground for human suffering; hence, the capacity for suffering of the class struggling to reproduce its physical existence is devalued. As compensation for the "slightest suffering," this class is presented with religion, as a compensation that has lost its force with the educated bourgeoisie; this class in turn requires more subtle forms of legitimation owing to the extent of secularization. At this point bourgeois art takes on a clear functional determination: it accomplishes for the bourgeoisie the task that is still best achieved by religion in the lower classes.

We ought to consider the thesis that the literary producers attempting to work on these needs, that is, to set up mass-market literature in opposition to literature as such, understand their activity primarily as affirmative in an undialectical sense. In contrast to the present-day culture industry, the authors in the era of gradually developing dichotomization of literature and the reading public are still aware of fulfilling a legitimation function within the expanding bourgeois-capitalist society.

The debate around popular texts can be understood as part of the struggle for the functional determination of literature beginning at the end of the eighteenth century. The documents analyzed here enable us to understand the inherent contradictions within the competing conceptions of literature of the period, those of the bourgeois Enlightenment and of autonomy; both are untenable in their exclusivity. When both parties argue against their own principles in the debate on popular texts, that is, when the advocates of autonomy praise these texts while the proponents of an Enlightenment-bourgeois concept of literature disdain them (to a certain degree at least), the limits of each conception become clear. The Enlighteners acknowledge the possibility that enlightenment might turn into counterenlightenment (and thus also the unsettling principle of evolution articulated by Adorno and Horkheimer in the *Dialectic of Enlightenment*); the elitist conception of those defending an aesthetic of autonomy lacks a reflection on the *real* reading needs of the new class of recipients, who desire satisfaction in the present world.[78]

A Concluding Remark on the False Sublation of the Dichotomy between Art and Life-Praxis

The reconstruction of the dichotomization of literature that I have attempted here demonstrates the two stages of the process.[79] A confirmed conservative politically, Salzmann still adheres to an Enlightenment concept of literature. He understands his literary activity as a contribution to the improvement of civil society and the novel as instrument of enlightenment. Despite a clearly normative purpose conveyed by an Enlightenment optimistic belief in the gradual dissemination of a rational global plan,[80] Salzmann's novel addresses a reader who is capable of criticizing prevailing normative systems and of rational solutions to social problems. It is precisely this conception of the Enlightenment novel whose addressee is an active recipient, however, that is attacked by the proponents of an aesthetic of autonomy, although they offer a positive evaluation of a certain type of popular text which encourages mere conformity and which finally erases that moment of involving the recipient as reflecting subject still present in Salzmann's work. This apparent paradox is resolved if one takes into consideration the fact that the dismissal of the Enlightenment novel and the well-intentioned toleration of a socially integrative mass-market literature for lower-class readers depends in turn on an oppositional conception of work and public. The institutionalization of literature as autonomous, which gradually penetrates society, must attempt to repress alternative institutionalizations—specifically that of the bourgeois Enlightenment—and banish them from social praxis. The institution of autonomy nonetheless establishes its own dichotomized system and sets aside a trivialized realm for the satisfaction of the "lesser" reading needs of a mass public.

In the historical contestation of the functional determination of bourgeois literature, the late-Enlightenment writers clearly could not sustain their own position in aesthetically persuasive terms. They had no historically progressive answers as to how the "threatening domination of the entertainment function in the bourgeois literature business could be broken through further developing or changing the material treated by novels."[81] Salzmann reacted to this situation by conforming to it and so becoming the forerunner in bourgeois mass-market literature. We can also see the tendency necessarily accompanying the aesthetic of autonomy, that of the false sublation of the separation of art and life-praxis. The literary elite withdrew from the task of cultivating the needs of the public and from the debate about the development of a concretely experienced bourgeois society. The great majority of literature consumers abandoned autonomous (high) literature, which denied them the satisfaction of practical needs. Excluded from an increasingly hermetic and remote culture, the broad public has been shunted in the direction of a limited array of mass-market texts served up by authors whose dependence on the market means that their professed response to the apparent needs of a mass public is no longer mediated by a critical-rational public sphere.[82]

Notes

1. On the strategy of the hack-writer [Lohnschreiber] charge in the fight against the radical Enlightenment opposition, see V. W. König, *Knigge und Knigge-Rezeption* (Staatsarbeit, University of Frankfurt, 1979).

2. R. Grimminger, "Roman," in *Deutsche Aufklärung bis zur französischen Revolution 1680–1789*, ed. R. Grimminger, part of *Sozialgeschichte vom 16. Jahrhundert bis zur Gegenwart* (Munich, 1980), 3/2:701ff. See also, for example, B. M. Beaujean: "Never before did the discrepancy between the absolute height of spiritual creation and profane commodities seem greater as during the 'Goethezeit'" (*Der Trivialroman in der zweiten Hälfte des 18. Jahrhunderts* [Bonn, 1964]).

3. The anti-Enlightenment affect of literary scholarship that adopts the doctrine of autonomy without reflecting on the historical conditions of its emergence and that makes this doctrine the foundation of an essential determination of the aesthetic is particularly clear in a study by Dieter Kimpel on the Enlightenment novel: "Translated into the understanding of the time, this means that even poetry is supposed to become the underling of a narrow-minded end

in itself, the human being; this end treats nature, the sciences, and the arts, indeed the plan of creation itself, as means for an immediate lease on life and attempts to use them as such" (*Der Roman der Aufklärung 1610–1774*, Sammlung Metzler 68 [Stuttgart, 1977]).

4. K.-J. Flessau, *Der moralische Roman. Studien zur gesellschaftskritischen Trivialliteratur der Goethezeit* (Cologne, 1968), 6.

5. E. D. Becker, *Der deutsche Roman um 1780*, Germanistische Abhandlungen 5 (Stuttgart, 1964).

6. F. Bouterwerk, "Geschichte der schönen Wissenschaften," in *Geschichte der Künste und Wissenschaften seit der Wiederherstellung derselben*, ed. a "Gesellschaft gelehrter Männer" (Göttingen, 1819), 2:382ff.

7. Peter Uwe Hohendahl and Jochen Schulte-Sasse, "Das Konzept bürgerlichliterarischer Öffentlichkeit und die historischen Gründe seines Zerfalls," in *Aufklärung und literarische Öffentlichkeit*, ed. Christa Bürger, Peter Bürger and Jochen Schulte-Sasse, Edition Suhrkamp, 1040 (Frankfurt, 1980), 84–111; see also the essay in the same volume by Christa Bürger, "Literarischer Markt und Öffentlichkeit," 162–212, as well as the introduction.

8. Christian Gotthilf Salzmann, *Carl von Carlsberg oder über das menschliche Elend* (1783–89; repr., Bern, 1977); future references are to the 1977 edition, and numbers refer to part and page. K. A. Ragotzky, "Über Mode-Epochen in der deutschen Lektüre" (1792; ed. W. Schmidt et al. and reprinted in *Journal des Luxus und der Moden* 1 (1970): 364ff.

9. For a contemporary polemic that places Salzmann's *Carlsberg* and "its ever more miserable successors" under the rubric of "novels of misery and suffering," which concedes the epochal character of the novel only to interpret away the rubric established with reference to the novel's content, see A. Koberstein, *Geschichte der deutschen Nationalliteratur*, ed. K. Bartsch (Leipzig, 1873), 4:235. Koberstein thus adopts the judgment (influenced by Goethe's notions of art) of the *Jenaische Allgemeine Literaturzeitung* (*JAL*) 4 (1795): 359ff.; here a novel modeled on Salzmann's is reviewed thus: "Salzmann's work has given rise to a number of moral-political novels, which have become progressively more remote from the completeness of their model." In *Deutsche Literaturgeschichte*, by A. Biese (Munich, 1917), 2:278, in a chapter entitled "Volkstümliche Literaturströmungenin der Zeit der Klassiker," Salzmann is dispatched in four lines as "the writer of a novel in which all human sins are described in their nakedness and sympathetic aspect." References to Salzmann's pedagogic activities (he was director of a reform school and was close to philanthropic ideas which he disseminated among farmers in a very effective weekly paper, *Der Bote aus Thüringen*) seem to me to be insufficient to explain Salzmann's expulsion from the canon of literature, even in the following cases: M. Beaujean (see n. 2) excludes *Carlsberg* from his study as a "work of an experienced pedagogue"; H. Boor and R. Newald, in *Geschichte*

der deutschen Literatur von den Anfängen bis zur Gegenwart (Munich, 1957), vol. 6, part 1, p. 193, mention Salzmann only as a student of Basedow; lastly, in the volume *Aufklärung* in *Erläuterungen zur deutschen Literatur*, ed. K. Böttcher and P. G. Krohn (Berlin/GDR; 1971), 697ff., Salzmann is dealt with not in the section on the Enlightenment novel but in a short chapter on philanthropy.

10. *Hamburgische unparteiische Correspondent* 182 (1783).

11. J. Schönert uses a "question/answer model" of the Enlightenment novel in a discussion of Johann Carl Wezel, "Fragen ohne Antwort. Zur Krise der literarischen Aufklärung im Roman des späten 18. Jahrhunderts," *Jahrbuch der deutschen Schiller-gesellschaft* 14 (1970): 183–229. Schönert, who describes his methodology as "content research," does not attempt to discuss the novels that he investigates in their historical context. Only in this way would significant statements about a "crisis in the Enlightenment" be possible.

12. Salzmann's novel contains scenes of such incomparable documentary value that it should be in every anthology on the Enlightenment. If we follow Erich Auerbach's remark that serious modern realism can only represent human beings embedded in a "concrete, continually evolving socio-politico-economic reality" (*Mimesis: The Representation of Reality in Western Literature*, trans. Willard Trask [Princeton: Princeton University Press, 1968], 443, trans. modified), then Salzmann has a place in the history of Western realism. See, for example, the scene in which von Brav, having lost his way in a storm, spends the night in a hut with a group of beggars and outcasts who tell him their stories of suffering (*Carlsberg* 3.166f.), or the episode in which the spectacle of soldiers running the gauntlet is enjoyed by high-ranking spectators on their balcony (3.331ff.), or the description of the torture chamber in the orphanage, where the "orphans' father" "improves" children who have not completed their mandatory work (1.349ff.), or the misery of the weavers exploited by the distributor (1.219f.).

13. Salzmann, *Carlsberg* 1.191.

14. See Salzmann's programmatic announcement of *Carlsberg* in Wieland's *Teutsche Merkur* (1783): "I came to the conclusion that if human knowledge, which has already got rid of a host of errors, can rid itself of certain others, human misery will come to an end and happiness will follow."

15. G. Klotz's claim that the radical social critique in the English novel of the 1790s (such as William Godwin's *Caleb Williams; or, Things as They Are*) can be explained in the context of already significant contradictions and misery in capitalist England is convincing; nonetheless the low estimation of this novel in Europe, as against the European enthusiasm for Richardson, cannot be explained in terms of a developmental gap between England and the Continent, if one takes into account that a conception of literary realism already existed in Germany in the 1780s; see R. Geissler et al., "Das Bild von Individuum und Gesellschaft im Roman," *Literatur im Epochenumbruch. Funktionen euro-*

päischen Literaturen im 18. und beginnenden 19. Jahrhundert, ed. G. Klotz et al. (Berlin, 1977), 166. The affinity between Salzmann's novel and Godwin's (see the preface to the latter, 1794) is astonishing. Proceeding from the insight that "the spirit and character of domination penetrates all social classes," Godwin claims that his novel offers "a general overview of the unreported force exercised in the domestic realm, by which human beings become their own destroyers" (William Godwin, *Caleb Williams; or, Things as They Are*, ed. David McCracken [New York: Oxford University Press, 1982], 1). For Godwin's views on literature, see D. McCracken, "Godwin's Literary Theory: The Alliance between Fiction and Political Philosophy," *Philological Quarterly* 49, no. 1 (1970): 113–33.

16. Quoted in *Empfindsamkeit*, ed. W. Doktor and G. Sauder (Stuttgart, 1976), 72.
17. Ibid., 76.
18. "A talented writer has an unlimited field of influence! Who can measure the limits of his influence! He speaks—nations listen. . . . Old, outdated prejudices collapse; reigning systems are transformed; peoples who were wandering in the dark see the light, and chains fall away from the feet of prisoners. The effect of the writer can often be felt in a thousand places simultaneously. The prince and the peasant, the scholar and the artisan, the old man and the child, the warrior and the tender mother, all at the same time in different places absorb his voice and feel its effects. As son of he who is alone immortal, the writer is effective for centuries, even for millennia" (Salzmann, Supplement to *Carlsberg* 5.186f). See also "The Editor to the Reader," *Carlsberg* 5.1f.
19. Quoted from G. Häntzschel, Foreword to reprint of *Carl von Carlsberg*, 11.
20. J. H. Merck, "Über den Mangel des epischen Geistes in unserm lieben Vaterlande" (1778), in *Ausgewählte Schriften zur schönen Literatur und Kunst*, ed. A. Stahr (1840; Göttingen, 1965), 178.
21. Similar attempts can be seen in drama; see O. Frel's remarks on rhapsodic drama, "Die Entstehung einer bürgerlichen Unterhantungskultur," in Bürger, Bürger, and Schulte-Sasse, *Aufklärung und literarische Öffentlichkeit*, 228ff.
22. Just how dominant the aesthetic of autonomy still is can be seen in new attempts at classification. Despite his positive treatment of Salzmann's narrative techniques, Häntzschel does not manage to abandon the charge of triviality. Still, *Carlsberg* is hailed as the predecessor of the "social critical novel"; see his Foreword to the reprint of *Carlsberg*, 33. The classification of *Carlsberg* in Grimminger's chapter on the novel for the *Sozialgeschichte der deutschen Literatur* has significant consequences for the as yet unchallenged (at least in literary scholarship) validity of traditional notions of evaluation and canonization. The very features praised in present-day literature—the dissolution of generic boundaries and formal experimentation (such as montage)—are criticized when found in Salzmann's work as "forced" and "artistic domination." Since conformism counts as a sign of triviality, and experiment is allegedly

always opposed to triviality, Salzmann's "formal originality" is cancelled by the reference to the "notable conventionality of the contents" (712ff.). We should be clear that "conventionality" in this context presumably includes the whipping of unwed mothers.

23. The positive evaluation of a novel with respect to its moral or Enlightenment influence together with the acknowledgment of the possibility of an aesthetic critique, which is nonetheless treated with a certain indifference, is typical of the reviews in periodicals of the late Enlightenment. See the review of *Carlsberg* in the *Hamburgische unparteiische Correspondenten* 182 (1783): "We note with pleasure the arrival of Mr. Salzmann's novel, which fully corresponds to our [i.e., the entire enlightened public's] expectations. . . . His moral stance has its own stamp of truth and utility. . . . The book contains a striking novel. . . . The main thread of the story, the treatment of which the critic may object to, does not make up the largest part of this wonderful work, since . . . the knots of the plot are not so utterly entangled."

24. See J. C. Wexel, *Kritische Schriften*, ed. A. R. Schmidt (Stuttgart, 1971), 1:4ff., and his Preface to *Herrmann und Ulrike*, ed. Eva Becker (Stuttgart, 1971), 1:5.

25. "Über den dramatischen Roman," in *Neue Bibliothek der schönen Wissenschaften und der freyen Künste* 44: (1791): 3–18; reprinted in *Romantheorie*, ed. E. Lämmert et al. (Cologne, 1971), 1:169, 170.

26. Ibid., 166.

27. Ibid., 165. The establishment of the novel on the basis of character and the categorization of incidents under the law of wholeness is discussed in the contemporary criticism; see Wilhelm Vosskamp, "Blanckenburg und Blanckenburg. Rezeption," in *Proceedings of the Fifth Germanist Congress, Cambridge, 1975*, ed. R. Forster et al. (Frankfurt, 1976), 2:195.

28. "Über den dramatischen Roman" (1791), 170.

29. Ibid.

30. Ragotzky's essay, "Über Mode-Epochen," 386ff., grasps very well, in a manner characteristic of the contemporary state-of-the-novel debate, both the details of the novel form tested by Salzmann and the grounds for its later rejection: "*Karl von Karlsberg* offers us a different tone. The novel has much to say about misery, but it does not so much whine as attempt to reason about removing it. This is a field in which our readers of trends might show themselves once again to be of strong mind. Much is said about reforming the world, about improving individual institutions, of purposeful education and the like. . . . I do not know whether six volumes of human misery were too much for one sitting, or whether one could sigh all the way through six volumes without reflecting rationally upon them, or whether Karlsberg went looking for misery in places that fashion never penetrates, or whether Karlsberg crammed many a truth into his skull: in short, the era of Karl Karlsberg will not last long."

31. The English social novel also had to defend itself against the accusation

of partisanship; on this subject, see Charlotte Smith's preface to *Desmond*: "Whoever takes umbrage at this matter will complain about the mode of portrayal and about the impropriety of making a light novel into an instrument of political debate" (quoted by R. Geissler, "Das Bild vom Individuum und Gesellschaft im Roman," 164).

32. "Über den dramatischen Roman," 171.

33. See Beaujean, *Der Trivialroman in der zweiten Hälfte des 18. Jahrhunderts*, 61 and passim.

34. Salzmann, *Carlsberg* 6.3.

35. Indeed, documents of the period suggest that writers debated the question of what would be meaningful in representing the world as it is, and whether it would be worthwhile to present a "catalogue of ten thousand evils" or to match "misery on earth" with "beautiful dreams" of a happy world, "visions" that a person needs to "act on the nerves," just as I need "Spanish wine to warm my stomach now and then," or, finally, "to join Voltaire's Candide in the garden to plant cabbage" ("Vom Übergewicht des Guten," *Teutsche Merkur* 63 [1788]: 388ff.).

36. Salzmann, *Carlsberg* 6.84. See also the editor's letter to the reader, 2.3ff.

37. See also *Carlsberg* 2.237, where one of the figures writes a letter, accusing a novelist of misrepresenting his otherwise "effective depiction of the confusion of the human heart" in such a way as to seduce a young girl. The novel "rights" this "wrong" through marriage.

38. See esp. Jochen Schulte-Sasse, *Die Kritik der Trivialliteratur seit der Aufklärung* (Munich, 1981), 52ff.

39. *Carlsberg* 2.6. Salzmannian realism has provoked a wide-ranging discussion which cannot be fully documented here. A few examples will have to suffice: *JAL* no. 246 (1790): 511f., reviewed a "countertext" to *Carlsberg*, *Justus Graf von Ortenberg. Ein Gemählde menschliche Glückseligkeit*, so as to remind its readers that "Mr. Salzmann all too often painted the real world too black." In Wieland's *Teutsche Merkur*, on the other hand, which did not, to my knowledge, review *Carlsberg*, the legitimacy of a realistic mode of writing was emphasized with clear reference to this issue; see "Über die Rechte und Pflichten der Schriftsteller," *Teutsche Merkur* 51 (1785): 199: "The world is not well served by untrue pictures that only represent the beautiful side of things while completely obscuring the faulty side or misrepresenting it through flattering embellishment." Gleim wrote a satirical poem, "Über Salzmanns *Carl von Carlsberg*": it was reprinted as an example of this "way of thinking" as late as 1804 in Kotzebue's magazine, *Der Freimütige* (no. 73). Gleim mocks a certain writer's fantasies of omnipotence and confronts them with the counterimage of a powerful ruler (Friedrich II of Prussia). The charge of "one-sidedness" was raised above all in the *Allgemeine deutsche Bibliothek*

68, no. 2 (1786): "Our writer does not seem to have any talent for judging the present from all points of view; he is almost always one-sided. . . . It seems to us that the writer has exaggerated somewhat, as is often the case."

40. Karl Philipp Moritz, "Das menschliche Elend," in *Schriften zur Aesthetik und Poetik*, ed. H. J. Schrimpf (Tübingen, 1962), 25.

41. Ibid., 27.

42. The attempt at an idealistic mollification of Salzmann's materialist perception of reality appears to be typical of his (pedagogic) working environment. See J. W. Ausfeld, *Erinnerungen aus dem Leben Christian Gotthilf Salzmanns* (Leipzig, 1884), 28: "[He recognized] that the chief source of suffering of so many people could be found within them."

43. Moritz, "Das menschliche Elend," 26.

44. Without "self-interest," "human striving would lose its *goad*, and the general competition its spur" (ibid., 25).

45. Ibid., 27ff.

46. Salzmann, *Carlsberg* 2.4, 11.

47. Ibid. 2.4.

48. Wilhelm von Humboldt, "Aesthetische Versuche 1," *Studienausgabe*, ed. K. Müller-Vollmer (Frankfurt, 1970), 1:48. Like Moritz and Humboldt, the writer of an anti-Carlsberg statement argued in 1790: "not everything is misery that looks like it. [The author] takes isolated incidents out of the context of the whole, which should always be more important to us, and treats those incidents as the scandal of humanity; although they may seem to be in isolation, such details are often not so in context" (Preface to *Justus Graf von Ortenberg. Ein Gemählde menschlicher Glückseligkeit* [Leipzig, 1795]).

49. Herbert Marcuse, "Über den affirmativen Charakter der Kultur," in *Kultur und Gesellschaft* (Frankfurt, 1968), 1:88; "The Affirmative Character of Culture," *Negations*, trans. Jeremy Shapiro (Boston: Beacon Press, 1969), 120, trans. modified.

50. In *Carlsberg*, written before the French Revolution, Salzmann is already vehemently opposed to the idea of popular sovereignty; the novel contains chapters that praise the enlightened despots (e.g., see 2.204ff.).

51. See, for example, the following reviews from the *Teutsche Merkur* (1785): 267ff., in which the critic classifies as members of a "writers' mob" those authors who take up the task of criticizing feudal power. The writer is "unscrupulous" toward the enlightener if he "hides his intelligence, for he can do no worse to oppressed subjects than making them more closely acquainted with their oppressor than the latter could do himself. . . . In so doing, the writer robs the common man of the soothing consolation that he bears no other load than the common good, takes away the consoling hope of finding justice, protection, and support from his lord, and gives him instead all the

torment of fear and hate." Indeed, Salzmann's critique does not target princes, only bad servants.

52. We can clarify this danger by looking at Moritz's theoretical position in the context of the contemporary debate. See, for example, the announcement of Schiller's magazine *Horen* in *JAL* (influenced by classicism) 1 (1795): 219. The magazine is praised for its refusal to publish contributions on politics and its intention to "offer to the readers of the *Horen*, which offers them spiritual succor, something that will take their attention away from the troubles and misery that they contend with daily, and enable them to feast their eyes on images of innocent people." The review of a family almanac in the same magazine offers a similar view: "Many people, wearied by the turmoil of political revolutions tossed out by the political journals, feel a need for different reading matter and long for depictions of domestic scenes and softer pictures that will help them forget wars and carnage." J. H. Merck, Goethe's friend from the Sturm und Drang period, mocks German authors in a letter to the editor of *Teutsche Merkur*, "Über den engherzigen Geist der Deutschen im letzten Jahrhundert" (1779); he accuses German authors of anxiety that frightens them away from a radical social critique: "We Germans . . . permit the love of art only in proper measure and only if nothing more important is lost!—one eats, drinks, and works at the appropriate time, and pays court to the girl in the evening—only if no errors are committed in the process" (*Ausgewählte Schriften zur schönen Literatur und Kunst*, 174).

53. See also Jochen Schulte-Sasse, *Literarische Wertung* (Stuttgart, 1976), 181.

54. *JAL*, no. 243 (1789), 395.

55. Ibid., no. 234 (1796).

56. Among other things, the success of R. Z. Becker's *Not- und Hilfsbüchlein* provides evidence for the need for enlightenment through literature. See R. Siegert, "Volksaufklärung und Buchhandelsstrategie um 1800. Zu R. Z. Beckers Bestseller 'Noth- und Hilfsbüchlein für Bauersleute,'" *Börsenblatt für den Deutschen Buchhandel* 44 (1980): B:305–16.

57. "Die Gesellschaft der Patriotischen zur Herausgabe der Universalbibliothek aller Wissenschaften und Künste vereinigten Literaturfreunde an das Publikum," in *Teutsche Merkur* 48 (1784): 185; see also "Über die Mittel, bessere Bücher in die Hände der niedrigern lesenden Menschenklasse zu bringen," in *Berlinische Monatsschrift*, ed. F. Gedike and J. E. Biester (1785), 295ff., and *Kaiserlich-privilegierter Reichsanzeiger* (1797), no. 76.

58. *JAL* 1 (1798): 152ff. (praises Salzmann's magazine, *Der Bote aus Thüringen* for its effective fight against prejudice).

59. A. von Knigge, "Über Schriftsteller und Schriftstellerei," (1793) in his *Schriften* (Hanover, 1804), 9:75ff. See also the review of this article in *JAL* 1 (1795): 531ff., which in this case defends artistic autonomy against Knigge. The battle

for the classification of "folk" literary forms, between forms oriented toward autonomy and those oriented toward life-praxis, continues well into the nineteenth century. See, for example, R. Gottschall's literary history, which gives Iffland and Kotzebue positive value as a counterinstitution to Weimar classicism, because they are related to Lessing and Diderot and because they write works which "intervene" "directly in contemporary social life" and raise the hope of a reconciliation of learned and popular literature (*Die Deutsche Nationalliteratur in der ersten Hälfte des neunzehnten Jahrhunderts*, 2 vols. [Breslau, 1855], 1:143ff.).

60. F. Bouterwek, "Idee einer Literatur," in *Neues Museum der Philosophie und Literatur* 2 (1804): 127ff.

61. J. F. Reichardt, "Freiheit für alle," *Deutschland* 1 (1796): 293. Reichardt attributes this division of humanity according to class to the "delusion" of the writers: "Nature has therefore condemned the larger part of humanity to service and deliberately granted it limited faculties? humanity consists therefore of simpletons and strong minds? . . . And that is supposed to be moral philosophy! I prefer to praise the traditional morality of Gellert, who speaks of the duty of *all* people to be clean and obedient" (294).

62. Review of Salzmann's *Sebastian Kluge* in *JAL*, no. 231 (1790).

63. J. G. Heinzmann, *Appell an meine Nation* (Bern, 1795), 111. Heinzmann is one of the most zealous anti-Enlightenment writers engaged in battle against the "reading flood," for whom the French Revolution and "novel reading" are two forms of the same corrupting development: "These two extremes have intertwined with each other, and it is not that improbable that novels have people and families as unhappy in private as the terrible French Revolution has made them in public" (139).

64. Knigge, in the *Hamburgischer unparteiischer Correspondent* (1796), no. 166. The review is particularly significant because it reveals how everything, including the ornamentation of these novels, is determined by the educational function and the addressee group. The reviewer hopes for a wide dissemination of the book, "that is appealing because of its clear print, finely worked engraving—a bust of Klausen, a shepherd in a rural setting, sitting under a tree with a book in his hand, accompanied by his flock, with Halberstadt in the background—and above all a good price." The ideological point of this image is clear: the farmer pictured here is rewarded by upward social mobility; in the background the city beckons with easier labor conditions.

65. Schlegel, in *Braunschweigisches Journal*, ed. E. C. Trapp (1790), 1.124: "Even so, the object ought to recommend the poem as useful and appropriate for expanding familiar sources of nourishment if not for opening new ones, and recommend it to our age that above all needs many active and, where possible, intelligent workers and noble men."

66. A. W. Schlegel, "Allgemeine Übersicht des gegenwärtigen Zustandes der deutschen Literatur," in *Über literatur, Kunst und Geist des Zeitalters*, ed. F. Finke (Stuttgart, 1974), 6.

67. "Über die Mittel, bessere Bücher in die Hände der niedrigern lesenden Menschenklasse zu bringen," 310ff.

68. The attack on Schlegel's position in the *Freimütige* [1803] no. 17, 65) is not groundless. According to the article, Schlegel's continuation of Tieck's work in "ennobling" the chapbooks could "lay the groundwork for a bibliography for the cultivated classes." What the *Freimütige* objects to is the fact that the Romantics appropriate the splitting of literature into serious and light literature, directed to respectively distinct social classes, without striving for a restoration of the unity of the institution of literature along the lines of an Enlightenment-bourgeois concept of literature.

69. Review of *Julchen Grünthal* in *JAL* 1 (1798): 253; also in A. W. Schlegel, *Sämtliche Werke*, ed. E. Böcking (Leipzig, 1846–47), 11:239.

70. Quoted by O. Fambach, ed., *Der Aufstieg zur Klassik in der Kritik der Zeit. . . . Ein Jahrhundert deutscher Literaturkritik, 1750–1850* (Berlin, 1959), 3:470. This volume also contains the documentation of the important argument between Schiller and Bürger.

71. The notion of readers' needs, which evinced a "merely physical hunger for novels" satisfied by "mass production" [*lose Waare*] that "never transcended mediocrity," was adopted by the Romantics as a self-evident social fact. The impact of their work was "therefore limited to the educated part of the public" (Review of the novels and short texts of F. Schultz by A. W. Schlegel in *JAL* 2 [1797]: 217ff.; see also the review of the collected stories of Marianne Ehrmann in *JAL* 4 [1795]: 200). A leitmotif of the contemporary criticism is the rejection of success as a measure of the aesthetic value of a literary work. For example, *JAL* stresses that "the sales figures of a book are irrelevant to its value and that nothing is more ridiculous than the bragging of certain bad or mediocre scribblers whose intellectual impoverishment is such that they seek the applause of the mob and attempt to combat the condemnation of connoisseurs by satisfying their publishers" (*JAL* 1 [1795]: 214ff.).

72. Criticism of mass-market literature typically appeared in the section on everyday life, as in *JAL*'s "Rubrik der Alltäglichkeit."

73. Christian Garve, "Über Moden," in his *Popularphilosophische Schriften über literarische, ästhetische und gesellschaftliche Gegenstände*, ed. K. Wölfel (Stuttgart, 1974), 1:383–555.

74. *Oberdeutsche allgemeine Literaturzeitung*, 3 March 1797, 418. The faults of a society subject to class scrutiny are also criticized in the *Journal des Luxus und der Moden* and examined in the context of a high stage of development in human culture; see S. Schütze, "Streifzüge um Markt, Kirche und Theater," in *Journal des Luxus und der Moden* 4 (1816–25): 241ff.

75. Salzmann, "Ankündigung," in *Kaiserlich-privilegierter Anzeiger* 168 (1706).

76. See R. Schenda, *Volk ohne Buch. Studien zur Sozialgeschichte der populären Lesestoffe, 1770–1910* (Munich, 1977), chaps. 1 and 2, and H. Klesel and P. Münch, *Gesellschaft und Literatur im 18. Jahrhundert* (Munich, 1977), chap. 2.

77. Salzmann's new novel offers a loose series of exemplary tales that are all supposed to prove the thesis that heaven can be found "here, on this much maligned earth, full of complaints, whining, whimpering, and gnashing of teeth," provided that the seeker has the right notion of "perfection": "Striving for perfection is almost universal, but it commonly takes the wrong road. This quest pursues externals instead of seeking inwardly. The common goal of human striving and action is more comfort, better nourishment, more satisfaction of bodily desire. Perfection as such is sought after only insofar as it serves as a means toward this main goal" (*Der Himmel auf Erde*, ed. E. Schreck [Leipzig, 1895], 7, 28).

78. A similar debate, in this case around the acknowledgment of a literature serving the practical needs of the broad masses of the population, also took place in France. See, for example, the article "De la nécessité d'étendre la littérature française," *Journal de Paris* 111 (1799), which calls on the well-known university critic La Harpe to offer a course on popular literature.

79. That the case of Salzmann is in no way a random individual case but rather one of historical significance can be seen in a parallel example. The evolution of August Lafontaine is determined by a similar break.

80. Contrast this with the disintegration of the Enlightenment novel in Wezel's *Belphegor* and the excellent analysis of V. U. Müller, "Aufklärung als 'traurige Wissenschaft,'" in *Reise und Utopie. Zur Literatur der Spätaufklärung*, ed. H. J. Piechotta, Edition Suhrkamp, 766 (Frankfurt, 1976), 170–221.

81. See O. Frels, "Die Entstehung einer bürgerlichen Unterhaltungskultur," in *Aufklärung und literarische Öffentlichkeit*, ed. Christa Bürger, Peter Bürger, and Jochen Schulte-Sasse (Frankfurt, 1980), 228.

82. See Jochen Schulte-Sasse's contributions to Bürger, Bürger, and Schulte-Sasse, *Aufklärung und literarische Öffentlichkeit*.

5

Classical Processes of Dissociation

Goethe's *Iphigenia*

It pains me that the king of Tauris should speak as if no stocking-weavers in Apolda were starving.

—Goethe

In the theater an audience, or a part of an audience, is put on display for another audience; this was apparently the Greeks' intention in using the chorus in tragic drama or the personification of the people individually or en masse in comedy. Theater and spectator belong together like image and reflection; their reciprocal effect is on and against each other; each is elevated and animated by the other.[1]

If we analyze the documents of *Götz von Berlichingen*'s initial reception (1773), we may claim that, with this early play, [J. W. von] Goethe reached that point of union with his audience that Herder refers to in the "letters on humanity."[2] At this point, the hope for a German national theater, evident since Lessing, acquires tangible shape. Herder's notion of such a theater is oriented toward the concept of influence [*Wirkung*], meaning the development not of an audience able to appreciate literature but of a national consciousness: "Brothers, let us pursue another way of judging plays, let us examine their consequences, their total impact . . . on the great divine good. . . . Let us not discard this book unused after the first reading, let us first reflect with an impassioned soul on the character of this ancient German and, if we find him to be good, make him our own, so that we can become Germans again."[3] The contemporary recipients of *Götz* spontaneously and almost unanimously (apart from the courts' rejection of the play; Friedrich II himself intervened in the discussion) grasped the political dimension of the new dramatic form. In choosing his material, Goethe decided *in favor of* bourgeois tragic drama and *against* rule-bound court tragedy.[4] A cross section of numerous documents of *Götz von Berlichingen*'s initial reception reveals the almost ideal correspondence between the work itself and audience expectations. Articulated in these documents is indeed something of what Habermas has tried to construct as "rational public sphere." In the era of Enlightenment, literature serves this public sphere as an instrument of consensus on social norms; this concept of literature emerges as literature comes to grips with its function as representation and diversion in court culture. With Goethe's *Götz*, the Enlightenment-bourgeois institutionalization of literature becomes the dominant form.

Goethe's work in the subsequent period represents a thoroughgoing engagement with this material: his return to doggerel in the *Urfaust* entails not only the formal renewal of a free, popular verse form but also a stylistic principle; this principle allows him to rework philosophical content in a literary way, using a popular form and a significant approximation of everyday speech, and thus to make this content, mediated by aesthetic pleasure, accessible to general discussion. If we follow Hegel in treating the work of art as the *expression* of the sociohistorical character [*Gehalt*] of a period, then we can read the *Urfaust* as an extremely clear-sighted answer to the central (normative) problems of a period of social upheaval, as a work that can be compared to *Le Neveu de Rameau*. At issue in the play is untimeliness [*Ungleichzeitigkeit*] and its tragic consequences, the collision of two worlds, the traditional feudal world to which Gretchen is tied and the modern bourgeois world of Faust. Old ties are loosened in the face of new levels of development; [the new] requires that the irrationality of tradition and authority be susceptible to the rational scrutiny of universalism, and that assumed norms yield to the autonomy of the subject.

At the same time, the historical significance of the play is that a hitherto socially unacknowledged fate is taken seriously and represented as human: Gretchen's suffering is the suffering of traditional society, which disappears with her. What emerges in the *Urfaust* is Goethe's incomparable ability to generalize collective experiences of suffering in aesthetic form and so to make those experiences conscious and accessible to articulation, available to the extent that Goethe falls back on popular formal traditions, in order to extend the subject matter of bourgeois tragic drama. Extension should not be misunderstood in immanently literary terms; in the

Urfaust the possibility of a national popular theater emerges, which could be likened to the theater of Lope de Vega or Shakespeare.

It is well known that Goethe broke off his work on the *Urfaust* when he moved to Weimar. Further, he did not publish the fragment. When he took up his literary work after many years of artistic abstinence, he started from a different position. With *Iphigenia*, Goethe returned to prebourgeois (courtly) subject matter; in so doing, he was well aware that he was alienating himself from his audience. There are only a few examples of this sort of break in the history of art. To explain it, we have to reconstruct the institutional limit conditions within which Goethe worked and within which his work was received. At issue, in this context, however, is not the conditions of production but the possibility of the present-day reception of the classics. The question is, therefore, what significance can be gleaned from a work like Goethe's *Iphigenia*? Only if we can still make the classics contemporary can we hope to overcome the crisis in historical consciousness. We can stand up to the current withering away of history only if potentially contemporary qualities [*aktualisierbare Gehalte*] in those works, which are threatened with oblivion, and which the bourgeois canon presents as classics, are sustained. We might, for example, consider an otherwise completely unrecorded, subversive history of the ego, as a history of resistance against the force of relations. The issue in the following discussion is whether the text of Goethe's *Iphigenia* allows itself to be deciphered as an aesthetic document of the early history of bourgeois subjectivity.

If we examine *Iphigenia* in the sociohistorical context of its genesis, we come across a phenomenon which could have the effect of a shock on a society like our own, characterized by the withering away of experience: the clearly scandalous discrepancy between the concrete wealth of Goethe's experience and the work's isolation from real life [*Wirklichkeit*]. That is the art of "the destruction of nature as real life" the suppression of "any disposition directed toward the knowledge of real life" in favor of form. This is Schiller's dream of the absolute work of art: "pure light, pure freedom, pure faculty, in which anything mortal is extinguished in a poetic representation." [5]

Hanns Eisler, whose adaptation of *Faust* engages the debate about the bourgeois heritage, seems to me to strike the central point of the reduction of art in the Weimar court when he makes the act of forgetting the most important condition in the pact with the devil. Faust, the bourgeois intellectual who longs for the peace of a good conscience, without which he has no strength for productive activity, must repress his own past, must forget the songs of the peasants whose cause he has betrayed. Goethe the writer must repress the experiences of his daily routine as a civil servant, the memory of the physical and moral wretchedness of the peasants and manufacturing workers in Saxony, the "moles" whom he must feed. So closely does reality dog him that, in order to be able to write, he seeks refuge in the intoxicating power of music. While he was writing *Iphigenia*, he had wine brought, and a quartet played in the next room.[6]

The ability of the bourgeois intellectual to persist in treating real life with the distance of contemplation, even at the point at which he would change or decisively influence it, maintains above all a moment of violence. "We climbed up high mountains and the pinnacle of the temple," writes Goethe, "there to gaze on the realms of the world and their hardship . . . and were surrounded by such illumination that the past and future privation and hardship of life lay like dross at our feet."[7] For Goethe, art, career, politics, cannot be conceived as a unity; all that he strives to maintain is the unity and intactness of his individuality. The price that he is ready to pay for this seems high—*alienation:* "pure, persistent alienation from humanity."[8] Goethe's autobiographical observation indicates the consciousness of an artist who experiences his relationship to society as problematic. Read in this way, *Iphigenia* makes the history of the bourgeois intelligentsia comprehensible as—guilty—alienation. That suffering loneliness, the price paid for forgetting, can be seen in the melancholy of the iambic rhythm. This is the basis of the pain which the artist can express—art protects us from despair:

> Die Träne hat uns die Natur verliehen,
> Den Schrei des Schmerzens, wenn der Mann zuletzt
> Es nicht mehr trägt—und mir noch über alles—
> Sie liess im Schmerz zur Melodie und Rede,
> Die tiefste Fülle meiner Not zu klagen.   (*Tasso*, 5.5)

> [That Nature gave us tears and cries of pain
> When man can bear his sufferings no more,
> She gave all that to you. To me she gave
> The added gift of melody and speech
> To rent my sorrow fully.[9]

The tragic hero's spiritual lyricism, in Lukács's terms, is not merely "the intoxication of the soul, gripped by destiny and transformed into song; it is also the torture of the creature condemned to solitude, while devoured by the longing for community. This loneliness gives rise to new tragic problems, the problem peculiar to modern tragedy: that of trust." [10]

Today, behind the endless flow of speech, flowing softly and seemingly smoothly in a classical manner, we can—at some distance—make out the producer's suffering. It is as though someone had to talk about his life, had to vindicate the fact that he kept silent about matters of which he should have spoken: "it pains me," Goethe wrote to Charlotte von Stein, the only person that he trusted, "that the king of Tauris should speak as if no stocking-weavers in Apolda were starving." [11] In his monologue addressed to her, he confesses that his artistic production stagnates to the point of complete paralysis, when he does not manage to repress the thought of the misery that he sees daily. Here, it seems to me, is the key to the contemporaneity of *Iphigenia*, as a part of the history of bourgeois subjectivity. The problematic of that history, experienced as the guilt-ridden link between emancipation and repression, lies in the possession of autonomy at the expense of the disenfranchisement of those excluded from this autonomy: the majority of humanity. The self-realization of the bourgeois subject carries with it the nonrealization of the excluded other.

The result of the exclusion of reality in favor of form, Weimar classicism is a national culture produced indirectly through art: it is classical not in the sense of expressing the identity of the nation but precisely in its radical aloofness and remoteness from its time, its indifference to the "limited interest of the present," even in cases where the present is governed by great revolution. Aesthetic culture, understood as a culture which "is forbidden any connection with *current* affairs and with the *immediate* expectations of humanity," is duty-bound only to a "higher general interest in what is *purely human* and elevated above any temporal influence." [12]

Our next question will be how the dissociation of art and praxis of life—which in Goethe's *Iphigenia* appears as paradigmatic—is established in the play itself. The first point is erasing the traces of artistic labor in the work:

Nicht der Masse qualvoll abgerungen,
Schlank und leich, wie aus dem Nichts gesprungen,
Steht das Bild vor dem entzückten Blick.

[Not painfully wrung from the masses,
But slim and light as though sprung from nothing,
Is the image before the enchanted gaze.

(Schiller, *Das Ideal und das Leben*)

But the power of repressed reality is betrayed in the anxious tension of classical form, in the precarious attainment of the organic work of art.

Life is not organically absent from modern drama; at most, it can be banished. But the banishment which classicists practice implies a recognition, not only of the existence, but also of the power of what has been banished: it is present in every word and every gesture which overreach themselves in anxious overextension in order to keep that banished life at bay, to remain untainted by it.[13]

The first version of *Iphigenia*, written in prose, did not satisfy Goethe's desire for art; with much effort, he produced a final rendition in verse. The touchstone for his reworking, for which he got scholarly advice, especially from [J. G.] Herder and [Karl Phillip] Moritz, was the concept of the harmonious: the verse form lends the play the strangeness that Benjamin called "aura," which corresponds to the distance from reality in the play's content. Wilhelm von Humboldt established very precisely the historical novelty of Goethe's *Iphigenia*: the metrical form grounds the autonomous status of the text, which ought to appear "strange" to the gaze tied to real life; the text has its place only in the realm of art. On the threshold of the nineteenth century, Humboldt distinguished between two possible institutionalizations of art, the touchstone for this distinction being art's connection to real life. What I have called the Enlightenment-bourgeois institution of art, Humboldt calls "prosaic" and "involved in life"; autonomous art, on the other hand, is "poetic" and "idealistic," in other words, separated from the praxis of life.[14]

The concealment of work in *Iphigenia* is expressed on the level of content in the radical degree to which language itself becomes an object. The potential for conflict in the play is based on the disturbance of relationships between people: on the one hand, relationships between kin (the house of Tantalus); on the other, relationships between strangers (the Scythians or barbarians vs. the Greeks, representatives of humanity). The ideal of humanity, which constitutes the content of *Iphigenia* in the traditional interpretation, can be understood in Habermas's terms as the construction of ideal communication, authentic and free from domination. Communication that is free from domination, even where it is represented as utopian, as a prelude to an ideal form of life, and not as actuality [*Wirklichkeit*], ought nonetheless to remain merely apparent reconciliation, insofar as its real conditions are left out. We might ask, in other words, how the classical ideal of humanity is mediated by the contradictions of the society out of which it has evolved.

These contradictions reappear in the work itself. Although he does not follow through his dialectic interpretation of the play to the point where it would be compelling, Adorno rightly notes that it is precisely the fragmentary quality of the ideal of humanity so represented and the contradictions left intact in the text, which guarantee the truth-value of that ideal for the contemporary recipient. Goethe's humanity is based on privilege; it is accessible only to an elite and paid for with the mute suffering of those excluded from this company. The aesthetic eloquence of the artist corresponds to the silence of the oppressed. The people have no voice in *Iphigenia*. The inhumane moment of this discriminating humanity is directly addressed in the play. Iphigenia abandons the Scythian people, despite her insight that the truth of humanity ought above all to be preserved in the dissemination of enlightenment among those in need of it. "The victims of the civilizing process, those who are oppressed by it and those who have to pay the price for civilization, are cheated out of its fruits, trapped in a precivilized state." [15] Iphigenia must repress her recollection of the Scythians, as Eisler's Faust had to repress his recollections of the songs of the Peasants' War. Adorno's interpretation of *Iphigenia* in light of the *Dialectic of Enlightenment* is a radical move to render it contemporary. Progress always also signifies repression and thus also guilt. Horkheimer and Adorno are concerned with explicating the dialectic of alienation and emancipation in all cases against Marx's denouement in a theory of revolution: "the external fate, in which human beings were entangled for the sake of emancipation from their natural decay is also their internal fate."

As Horkheimer and Adorno, who are indebted to Freud, repeatedly emphasize, the "domination over non-human nature and over other human beings" was paid for with the "disavowal of nature in human beings." "This very disavowal, the nucleus of all civilizing rationality, is the germ cell of a proliferating mythic irrationality; with the disavowal of nature in human beings, not merely the telos of the outward

control of nature, but also of human life itself is distorted and be-
fogged. As soon as human beings cut themselves off from their awareness that they are themselves nature, all the goals for which they live—
social progress, the intensification of all material and spiritual powers,
even consciousness itself—are nullified and the enthronement of the
means as an end, which under late capitalism is tantamount to open
insanity, is already perceptible in the prehistory of subjectivity." . . .
The subjection of nature in human beings [is] the primary condition
of personal autonomy: it belongs to the developmental mechanism
of ego-identity. The consequences of the world-historical identity of
both processes is, however, that the subjects have become reified to the
same degree as objects in external nature.[16]

The dialectical philosophy of history enables us to sharpen our focus on
the structure of the contradictions in *Iphigenia*. Language in this play is
unequally distributed: the language of the servant class bears the sign of
instrumental reason and is marked by calculation, reified like the consciousness of the society in which its members are absorbed. Authenticity
is the province of the rulers, whose speech is not subjected to alien purposes and does not serve the maintenance and reproduction of their own
existence; its criterion is not success, but truth. Having speech at one's disposal signifies the possibility of autonomy, of liberation from traditional
ties. This autonomy too is inaccessible to the others.

The contradiction in the opposition between Greeks and barbarians is
expressed in the plot. Humanity and its historical evolution are constituted
as Greek in the play, that is, as exclusive and discriminating. The opposition enables the dramaturgical resolution of the play and simultaneously
reveals its ideological character. Humanity is grounded in the exchange of
what are only ostensible equivalents: truth for truth, friendship for friendship. But only the barbarian Thos is obliged to relinquish both the power
and love, which alone guarantee for him the meaning of human conduct
and also the security granted by tradition.

Classicism as a process of exclusion. I have suggested which concrete
experiential possibilities Goethe had at his disposal; he was acquainted—
more precisely than most intellectuals of his time—with the misery of the
working population, which was the underside of emergent bourgeois society. Contrary to his own experience, he organized the plot of *Iphigenia*
as if the humanizing process needed only to overcome the inner resistance

of the subject. In my view, this is the function of the myth of the house of Tantalus, a myth that constitutes the epochal value of the play. The house of Tantalus can be understood as the side of inner human nature, which in the course of human history has been only incompletely brought under control: the residual barbarism and rebellion that remains when the rational self of humanity splits off from the natural self.

The members of this house have to escape captivity in an archaic world of drives, passions, and violence. The last members, Orestes and Iphigenia, are supposed to succeed in this leap from myth into history. Martin Walser is right to speak of Iphigenia's "leap into the purely true" as an act that "can be achieved only in a rootless, and nicely monochrome Weimar." For morality which is grounded on trust and on a consensus achieved by speech in a site free from domination lacks secure foundation, because the question about the interest that sets the civilizing process in motion is not posed. Where do brother and sister get the need for truth and authenticity, which they express in dramatic form? On what material basis does the humanity—which they have provided with language—rest, while in the domain of work underneath, all is silent? "Showpiece for humanity" or "humanity without society or without history, or, worse still, humanity against history"?[17] The ideological moment in Goethe's solution becomes clearer when compared with Diderot's *Neveu de Rameau*: in that text, the problems emerging in modern society in the process of dissociation from traditional world pictures are not repressed. Rather, Diderot clearly lays out the aporias in the legitimation problematic of bourgeois morality. He pushes the discussion of the question as to the existence of a foundation for moral conduct, which does not conflict with the agent's interests, to the point where the Enlightenment project itself and its optimistic faith in progress cannot but seem threatened.[18]

The dissociation of art from the praxis of life, of which Goethe's *Iphigenia* is the earliest but also the most radical example, must obviously have consequences for its reception. As a bourgeois writer, working nonetheless under conditions of a kind of patronage in the aristocratic society of the Weimar court and from the political perspective of a compromise between nobility and bourgeoisie, Goethe looked for a kind of work whose significance would be overcome by the courtly institutionalization of art—if we assume that its functional determinants are representation and diversion. Nonetheless, the new aesthetic of autonomy developed by Goethe leads directly to the exclusion of the domain of work and political domination, which, in contrast to the courtly aristocratic way of life, belong essentially to the bourgeois individual's praxis of life.

The contradiction that marks Weimar classicism leaves traces not only in the works themselves but also in the distinctly dichotomous structure of the institution of literature at the turn of the nineteenth century. As in classical theater generally, the language of *Iphigenia* bears the stamp of discrimination and exclusion. Unlike the Enlightenment writer, the Weimar writers are not concerned with popularity but rather with a restricted focus on an educated elite. In conversations with [J. P.] Eckermann, Goethe expresses the conviction that "everything great and wise" exists only "in the minority." He cannot conceive that reason might become popular: "My works cannot be popular; whoever thinks so and pursues that aim is wrong. They are not written for the masses, but rather for the singular human being." [19]

The reception of classical literature presupposes what was called "higher education" in the nineteenth century: education that elevated one above the "popular." At Weimar, Goethe did not address the public of his time but, rather, a future public, on the way to being educated in the manner of Schiller's aesthetic education. Establishing the autonomy of literature exacted a high price: abandoning the possibility of shaping the normative determination of the bourgeois public sphere. The bourgeois reading public in the nineteenth century, which adhered to the practical function of literature, did not at first accommodate art's claim to autonomy and rejected works that did not satisfy their need for normative orientation. This development can be examined from two angles: on the one hand, the work's interest for recipients was displaced onto the artistic personality (visible especially in the Goethe cult), and on the other, the majority of the recipients turned toward literature hitherto excluded as "low." Up to now, we have lacked a differentiated instrument of literary analysis—Adorno's historicophilosophical interpretation in *Dialectic of Enlightenment* seems exemplary to me—in order to establish the humanistic character of a play, from which we are separated by more than mere temporal distance. Reconstructing the historicity of this play in particular has already unearthed a series of difficult methodological problems, as we have seen.

The dichotomy between educated elite and literary consumers, between reflective and deficient appropriation, corresponds to the dissociation of high and low literature, visible since the end of the nineteenth century. The unity of a national literature only recently won manifests itself as contradictory already in the moment of its creation: the fine continuity of an ever-advancing bourgeois literature, from Gellert and Gottsched through Lessing to Goethe and Schiller comes unstuck in the dichotomy between high and low, art and commodity, canon and trivia, education and entertainment. Against the writers Goethe and Schiller are flanked the theater men Iffland and Kotzebue.

Reading Goethe's *Iphigenia* today cannot mean laying bare its humanistic character. On the contrary, one would almost prefer to say that what is expressive of Goethe's period in *Iphigenia*, as it emerges in the collision between the classical text and the philosophy of tragedy in *Dialectic of Enlightenment*, has to do precisely with the fragmentary quality of the work. Here the ideal world of humanity appears as not simply available but apparently in contemplative veneration. A violent learning process has the advantage over contemplation: the myth of the house of Tantalus, present everywhere in the classical oeuvre, cannot be fully banished into prehistory; it keeps alive the memory of the inseparable link between human culture and domination, violence, and oppression. Demonstrating this link in the play is the mute but tangible opposition between Greek human beings and Scythian barbarians. The peculiar freedom of these "Greek bandits" owes its existence to the "surplus of history already produced," accomplished with the efforts of autochthonous peasant peoples.[20] The construction of humanity rests on the work of those who are at the same time excluded from it.

So the truth of the drama lies in the extent to which it allows us to recognize the victims of these moments out of phase with historical time. For peoples and, in the history of bourgeois society, classes as well, emerge from prehistory at different social rates; the variation in this rhythm of progress produces collective and individual suffering. Goethe's Iphigenia, bearer of the idea of humanity, knows the price of progress and is ready to pay it. We have here a literary work in which the problematic aspect of the development of bourgeois culture in Germany emerges clearly. The text is significant, because it is here that the producer's bad conscience rebels against his aesthetic intention. Pure form indeed, but not quite completely removed to "those regions of light" where "woe's turbid stream no longer sounds" (Schiller, *Das Ideal und das Leben*). *Iphigenia* thus stands

Christa Bürger

at the beginning of the bourgeois institution of art, while simultaneously offering the resistance of the individual work against that institution as a henceforth irretraceable sign of artistic achievement.

Notes

1. Johann Herder, "Haben wir noch das Publikum und Vaterland des Altens?" *Briefe zur Beförderung der Humanität*, ed. von H. Kruse (Berlin, 1971), 1:301, 57th letter.
2. See Christa Bürger, *Der Ursprung der bürgerlichen Institution Kunst*, esp. the introduction and chaps. 1 and 7.
3. J. M. R. Lenz, "Über *Götz von Berlichingen*," in Hans Mayer, ed. *Meister-werke deutscher Literaturkritik* (Berlin/DDR, 1954), 1:297.
4. The following qualification is relevant here: the decision in favor of specifi-cally bourgeois subject matter does not entail an antifeudal political position on Goethe's part. The play *Götz* unambiguously opposes the rebellious farm-ers, and the figure of Götz recalls prebourgeois ways of life. Feudal rank is engraved on Götz's world and nostalgically celebrated by Goethe.
5. See Wilhelm von Humboldt, *Studienausgabe*, ed. K. Müller-Vollmer, Fischer, 6040 (Frankfurt, 1970), 1:44, 55. Also see *Briefwechsel zwischen Friedrich Schiller und Wilhelm von Humboldt*, ed. S. Seidel (Berlin/DDR, 1962), 1:243.
6. See *Goethes Briefe an Frau von Stein*, ed. K. Heinemann (Stuttgart), 1:142 (letter of 6 March 1779); 1:139 (letter of 22 February 1779); 2:34ff. (letter of 8 September 1780); 2:37 (letter of 9 September 1780). For Eisler's reception of *Faust*, see his unfinished opera, *Johann Faustus* (1952).
7. Goethe to Charlotte von Stein, 21 September 1780, *Goethes Briefe*, ed. K. R. Mandelkow and B. Morawe (Hamburg, 1962), 1:322ff.
8. *Goethes Tagebuch aus den Jahren 1776–1782*, ed. R. Keil (Leipzig, 1875), 150.
9. Goethe, *Tasso*, trans. John Prudhoe (Manchester, 1979).
10. Georg Lukács, *Die Theorie des Romans* (Neuwied, 1965), 40; *The Theory of the Novel*, trans. Anna Bostock (Cambridge, Mass., MIT Press, 1971), 45, trans. modified.
11. Goethe to Charlotte von Stein, 6 March 1770, in *Goethes Briefe* 1:142.
12. Schiller, *Ankündigung der Horen*, in *Sämtliche Werke* 5:870.
13. *Theory of the Novel*, 43, trans. modified.
14. Humboldt, in a letter to Schiller, 26 March 1796, *Briefwechsel zwischen Fried-rich Schiller und Wilhelm von Humboldt* 2:56.
15. T. W. Adorno, "Zum Klassicismus von Goethes *Iphigenia*," in *Noten zur Liter-atur*, ed. Rolf Tiedemann, Bibliothek Suhrkamp, 395 (Frankfurt, 1974), 4:23.

16. Albrecht Wellmer, *Kritische Gesellschaftstheorie und Positivismus*, Edition Suhrkamp, 336 (Frankfurt, 1969), 139ff. Wellmer's citation is from Max Horkheimer and T. W. Adorno, *Dialektik der Aufklärung* (Amsterdam, 1947), 70ff.; *Dialectic of Enlightenment*, trans. John Cumming (New York: Continuum, 1972), 54, trans. modified.

17. Martin Walser, "Imitation oder Realismus," in *Erfahrungen und Leseerfahrungen*, Edition Suhrkamp, 109 (Frankfurt, 1965), 76ff.

18. See Peter Bürger, "Moral und Geschichte bei Diderot und Sade," in *Aktualität und Geschichtlichkeit*, Edition Suhrkamp, 879 (Frankfurt, 1977), 48–79.

19. J. P. Eckermann, *Gespräche mit Goethe*, ed. K. Ritschel and G. Seidel (Berlin/DDR, 1956), 450, 421. That this is no isolated comment is clear in the exchange of letters between Goethe and Schiller as well as in their collaboration *Xenien*. Schiller's polemic against G. A. Bürger is also extremely important in this context.

20. Alexander Kluge and Oskar Negt, "Der antike Seeheld als Metapher der Aufklärung," in *Stichworte zur "Geistige Situation der Zeit,"* Edition Suhrkamp, 1000 (Frankfurt, 1979), 1:138.

6.

Preliminary Remarks

"The natural and reasonable point of departure for literary study is the interpretation and analysis of literary works themselves."[1] This apparently unproblematic assertion is challenged by literary scholarship grounded in institutional-sociological analysis.[2] The issue here is the status and function or functional transformation of literature and the claim that the production and reception of literary works is determined by epochal limit conditions. The institutional framework in turn governs specific dealings with literary works, such as literary history, literary criticism or pedagogy, and interpretation. Seen from an institutional-sociological perspective, interpretation itself becomes the object of investigation. At issue in this essay, then, is not an interpretation of Kleist's *Erdbeben in Chili* [*Earthquake in Chile*] but rather an outline of the functional transformation of narrative at the beginning of the nineteenth century. The key question would therefore be: is it possible to interpret changes in the realm of narrative fiction in the context of the general transformation of literature at the turn of the eighteenth to the nineteenth century?

The functional transformation of literature at the end of the eighteenth century can be shown with reference to the concept of utility. According to the notions of progress in the Enlightenment, moral education is closely linked to the mastery of nature and aesthetic experience. It is precisely the irrational character of art, which represented for the Enlighteners a potential threat to social life based on reason, that becomes the point of departure for an instrumentalization of art as a means of "educating humanity." This bourgeois conception of norms and self based on utility becomes central in the Enlightenment institution of literature. The bourgeois-autonomous institution of art/literature, on the other hand, excludes utility from the realm of art. The beautiful becomes the counterprinciple of the "ruling idea of the useful" (Karl Philipp Moritz), and purposelessness becomes the decisive characteristic of the work of art.[3] Institutional-sociological literary scholarship departs from traditional scholarship in that it does not treat the conception of artistic autonomy as the essence of art but rather as a historically given framework. This departure is possible because historical avant-garde movements challenged the framework of autonomy.

Statement of the Problem

I would like to begin with a contemporary document of reception. *Das Erdbeben in Chili* is known to be one of Kleist's earliest stories; it appeared first in one of the most popular contemporary magazines, in Cotta's *Morgenblatt für gebildete Stände* [*Morning paper for the educated classes*], and then shortly thereafter in a volume of Kleist's stories. These *Erzählungen* were reviewed by Wilhelm Grimm in the *Zeitung für die elegante Welt* [Newspaper for the world of elegance]:

> The stories that Kleist has made available to the public are in no way French but rather thoroughly German, and thus more effective. . . .
> To be sure, they are not written for the masses, who want nothing more than sentimental love stories or trivial scenes from everyday life, decked out with general ruminations and moral instructions or foolish adventures born of a feverish imagination. In Kleist's stories, everything is out of the ordinary, in the content and plot as well as the incidents, but this extraordinariness is always natural and not merely there for its own sake, . . . [and so a fine means of] strengthening every vigorous spirit and broadening and elevating the view constrained by the habits of everyday life. This portrayal has no need of wretched aid from the ruminations and instructions that the common storytellers use to try to prop up their lifeless products.[4]

At first glance, this document of reception offers no particular interpretive difficulties. Wilhelm Grimm argues from the perspective of the aesthetic of autonomy, distinguishing "high" from "low" literature with the intention of separating Kleist from the horde of mass-market writers and of demonstrating the artistic character of his stories. His point about the social ranking of the audience is clear: in contrast to the "common storytellers,"

Kleist (the "true" artist, to elaborate on the counterconcept) writes not for the masses (of vile disposition) but for the educated classes ("vigorous spirit").

Nonetheless, the review is manifestly contradictory in its treatment of content and reception attitude. It appears that Grimm's evaluations change, depending on the system on which he focuses: morality and adventures appear in a negative light in the realm of mass-market or light fiction [*Trivialliteratur*] but in a positive light in the realm of art. In order to distinguish Kleist from mass-market writers, Grimm juxtaposes "extraordinary incidents" against "trivial scenes from everyday life," but runs into trouble at this point, since adventures provide the fundamental ground for mass-market literature. He therefore adopts a "higher" sort of adventure which he represents as "natural" and purposeful ("not there merely for its own sake"). In doing so, however, Grimm abandons a central category of the aesthetic of autonomy, for which purposelessness is *the* characteristic of the work of art. Introducing the category of the natural at this point not only suggests the hidden normativity of Grimm's concept of art but also alerts us to the second contradiction in his text. "Moral instructions," that is, the very connection to morality, are characteristic of light fiction. Nonetheless, Grimm still attributes to Kleist's stories a thoroughly moral influence, which is also explained as a form of higher morality. The demand for idealization (superelevation postulate), characteristic of the aesthetic of autonomy, especially in the work of the so-called popular aesthetic commentators, can be seen in terms such as "refresh," "strengthen," "elevate," "expand." In the determination of influence and reception attitude, the borders between light fiction and art have become completely fluid.

To dismiss this contradictoriness as the analytical weakness of the critic Wilhelm Grimm would not do justice to the problem that is concealed within it. Two points can be made here. First, the dichotomy between "high" and "low" at least in this period is difficult to establish in rational terms, since it is based on statements such as "Kleist *is* an artist." The investment of the work of art with aura [*Auratisierung*] apparently demands a counterprinciple. The institution of art excludes the trivial as nonart. Second, Grimm's review points to the central contradiction of the aesthetic of autonomy: it conceives of art and morality as two distinct realms, while elevating art on the grounds of its moral qualities.[5]

The review contains a further indication that can help us to answer the question of the functional transformation of art: the opposition between

French and German manners. Grimm would like to counter the prevailing opinion that French writers had the advantage over their German colleagues in the "subject matter of stories," "because they were already at home in an already existent nation, to which we have still to transport ourselves with the aid of art."[6] The argumentation here is also contradictory. The steps are as follows: the tale [*conte*] is a medium of social life; in Germany we have no literary public sphere, no education in society. Nonetheless, German stories are better because they originate in the "individuality" of the single artist.[7] Once again a lack is reinterpreted as a positive value; the argumentative figure that achieves this reinterpretation is the appeal to something "higher."

Ceci n'est pas un conte [This Is Not a Tale]

At this point, we come up against the program hidden in Grimm's review. The limitation of prose genres appears to be its arrangement in a communications context oriented toward normative discussion, precisely that on which the interest of Enlightenment prose narrative rests. Grimm rejects a functional determination of narrative conceived as medium for an "already existent nation," that is, as a medium for a literary public sphere. The new, German, indeed Kleistian way of telling a story "overcomes" this limitation. Grimm's concealed program stands in opposition to the Enlightenment-bourgeois concept of literature. Since Diderot's tales of the 1770s can be seen as paradigmatic of Enlightenment narrative, the function of this kind of narrative will be examined against them.

The research on Diderot can best be traced in the emphasis on the relationship between Diderot's *Contes* and the journalism of the early Enlightenment. As a part of the Enlightenment project, these stories have the following characteristics: they neglect the instance of originality (we might recall in contrast the dominant role later played by the "extraordinary incident" in the program of the German novella) in favor of the construction or reworking and connection of already-known, experienced, witnessed, events or stories. Moreover, they are oriented toward affect. The goal of the construction is to agitate the recipient, which the Enlightenment writers considered to be the necessary condition for the reflection on the social circumstances connected to the story. Diderot's *Contes* calls for the title that Hermann Broch gave to one of his novellas: *Methodologische Novelle* (1933); like Broch's novella, Diderot's tales are methodologically constructed and "represent one solution picked at random from the plethora of possible solutions."[8] Diderot's demand for a connection between an exemplary plot development and details from everyday life, the confrontation of norm and characteristic deviation, should be understood as a call for experimental narrative.

Dialogue is fundamental for Diderot's methodological tale. This corresponds to the tendency of the Encyclopedists to keep a certain distance from events, phenomena, and persons to enable them to question everything. Dialogue provides Diderot with the opportunity to mediate the most disparate elements. For it is in the medium of conversation that reality can be experienced as a collective construction in which the fragments of a conceived reality can be integrated with dream vision and the fantasies of madness. Reality emerges in experimental narrative and discussion as human labor. This program is also fundamentally distinguished from the idealist aesthetics operating in Grimm's review, since the issue is not the idealization of reality but rather its reworking.

Dialogue as fundamental principle of Diderot's *Contes* is more than artistic technique. Inventing stories is not so important. The tales are "methodologically constructed" in that they display whichever function befits the tale and suggest ways of dealing with stories. The dialogue partners of Diderot's narrators often already know the story and have already judged it. The story is told so that they can make sense of an event or an action—through reasoning and conversing—and so come to a judgment. Diderot's reader, the dialogue partner of his stories, expects no surprising turns, no "extraordinary incident," but rather a particular judgment of human action. The dialectic of dialogic narrative consists of the confrontation between judgment based on the perception of merely superficial phenomena evaluated by "common sense" (that of the listener) and the reflective judgment of the enlightened man (the narrator). In *Ceci n'est pas un conte*, two contrasting stories are told: in both cases, lovers sacrifice means, outward appearance, and health to the beloved, only to be abandoned by them. In the "commonsense" view, the beloved ought to appear as ungrateful, cruel, and calculating. Nonetheless, the narrator manages in the course of a process of discussion accompanying the story to unsettle the prejudice of the listener's abstract concepts. At the end of the *conte*, the question as to who is the victim and who is the guilty one remains open. The abstractness of the initial moral judgment is corrected by a reflection that examines the concrete, social-historical conditions of human action.

Originating in the era of transition from traditional to modern society, Diderot's stories can be understood as tools of the difficult learning process whose result ought to be the moral autonomy of the subject. The method in the tales is echoed in Hegel's cunning little essay of 1807, *Wer denkt abstrakt?* [*Who thinks abstractly?*]. Hegel also suggests that the solution to questions raised in an enlightened society should be found through conversation. The point of Hegel's essay is thus the reverse of a common prejudice. The prejudice consists of the idea that there is a hierarchy in the conceptual as well as the social world and thus privileges the abstract concept at the expense of "common" sense, which is in turn based on concrete observation. Hegel juxtaposes this value opposition to social reality by attributing abstract thought (which he treats as lower) to the common man and concrete thinking to the educated. Thus he intends to show what dialectic is: engage with the matter at hand. The examples that he develops are likewise models of Enlightenment narrative:

Thus a murderer is brought before the seat of justice. For the common people, he is no more than a murderer. Ladies might perhaps notice that he is a stronger, handsomer, more interesting man. The people, however, find this observation shocking. . . . A priest, who knows the basis for things and hearts, might add that this is characteristic of the moral corruption prevalent among their "betters."

Someone who understands human beings looks for the path taken in the criminal's education, finds in the story of his bad upbringing and the relationship between his father and mother some extremely harsh response to a trivial mistake of this man, which embittered him against the bourgeois order and which drove him from it. . . .

To think abstractly is to see in the murderer only the abstract idea that he is a murderer and thus to reduce all remaining human essence to this simple quality.[9]

Secret History

Telling stories is an integral element of philosophical demonstration: the example of Hegel seems to me appropriate for demonstrating the astounding wealth of Enlightenment narrative forms and for pointing to the fact that the tradition of the experimental, reflective tale is in no way limited to France. That the problematization rather than the mediation of bourgeois normative conceptions is at issue here should also be clear. Given the crisis in the autonomy of art, we can agree that something was lost when the function of narrative shifted from enlightenment to autonomy, namely, the possibility of collectively working through social problems in the public medium of literature.

I would now like to examine Kleist's narrative within the context of this functional transformation. First, we ought to see not only his contributions to the *Berliner Abendblätter* but especially the novellas in the tradition of the crime story and the horror story. In order to articulate this problematic, I will return once more to Hegel's essay. For Hegel, there is a third group situated between common sense and educated society, whom he doubts can be enlightened: the readers of the *Morgenblatt für gebildete Stände*, which takes an undesirable interest in the criminality of the day. They fall prey to the opposite abstract in that they strew flowers on the wheel to which the criminal is bound. To Hegel, this represents a "reconciliation in the mode of Kotzebue, a kind of dissolute accommodation of sensibility along with the bad." [10]

The aesthetic validation of the crime story as a genre is in Germany usually associated with Schiller. In his foreword to the German version of "Merkwürdige Rechtsfälle als ein Beitrag zur Geschichte der Menschheit [Remarkable legal cases as a contribution to the history of humanity]" (1792), Schiller attempts to justify the German translation with the following argument: one ought not to abandon the satisfaction of the needs of new classes of readers to "mediocre scribblers and publishers in search of profits" but should rather employ the general desire for "passionate and complicated situations" "to nobler ends." Schiller defines this end as "knowledge of human beings and how to treat them," which can be developed through conversation. For the Enlightenment Schiller, the important thing is above all *how* these cases are related in a manner that might communicate to the reader the "ambiguity of the decision that often embarrasses the judge." [11]

It may surprise us that Schiller at no point mentions the work of a writer (now forgotten) who was very well known at the time and whose *Skizzen* [Sketches] published after 1778 would have corresponded exactly to Schiller's own ideas. August Gottlieb Meissner collected this kind of legal case and—in accordance with his Enlightenment conception of literature—used a variety of minor forms in reworking these cases: anecdote, fable, dialogue, letters, and so on. He always demanded collaboration from his reader. He understood his *Skizzen* as a way of provoking discussion for an enlightened public or one in the process of enlightenment. Meissner also reflected on the function of the narration of (lived, heard, read) actual incidents. He regretted that the public took notice only of the fate of those outlaws elevated by rank or pedigree, rather than the many anonymous ones:

> How often would we encounter in the criminal files of a dusty court chamber many an incident that gives us better insight into the *secret history* of the human heart than the volumes of so-called keen observers of human nature. How often would we see the power of vice and virtue tightly entwined and so admire or at least lament the very one whom we had despised only a short while before. . . . how doubtful would we often be when we had to decide whether the deed that human laws punish with death and ought indeed to so punish would appear as barbarity or nobility in the eyes of the world.[12]

For Meissner's narrator, as for Diderot's, the issue here is the problem of judging human actions. He presents examples "mixing good and cruelty." It would not be fair to Meissner to see in this only an attachment to the Aristotelian demand for a compound character. His interest is rather in legal cases which are said to shake a secure sense of abstract evaluations of people and their fate.[13]

The concept of the "secret history" that Meissner develops in his narrative program had the effect of establishing a tradition. Indeed, the program contains much that is characteristic of the Enlightenment: the possibility of an everyday (hi)story, put together from the experiences and fortunes of common people, as material for public rational discourse [*Räsonnieren*]. Achim von Arnim uses the concept in this sense in his novella cycle *Der Wintergarten* (1808). In this cycle, he uses an episode from the chronicle by Froissart, whom he praises as an exemplary historiographer because he "treated history as memory in the mode of Herodotus and offered [Arnim] an example of a secret history of [his] time that must yet be written." [14] The eyewitness reports from which this secret history of the era can be assembled do not have the status of elevated works of art; they are also not published singly but rather as stories in accounts in almanacs or as anecdotes, exempla, or crime reports in magazines; the former were read primarily by the rural population and by artisans, whereas the latter were read by "educated people of all ranks" in the cities. A growing need for this kind of story can be seen emerging after 1789; at the same time one may note that the dialogic moment is exceptionally developed.[15] These are stories which are read, discussed, used, and reflected on in conversation.

At issue here is not the resuscitation of a forgotten literature on the basis of its apparent popularity or the glorification of the almanac as the expression of a real history from below. Nonetheless, we ought to be able to see that an important element of the Enlightenment lives on in the narrative genres of the magazines or is at least potentially, latently present. We should remember Herder's *Adrastea*, a polemic against the autonomy of art, in which memoirs and maxims are understood as the fundamental form of human community: "*Life* is the expression of the agent's power; the tongue, helm of reason, would *speak* of whatever affects soul and hand. It is through *speaking of himself* that the actor enlightens himself." [16] Herder explicitly calls for each individual to give an account of his own life to himself and the public at large; for only through truthful examination of individual and social conditions of evolution can the "oppressive obstacles in the way of human development [*Bildung*] be removed." "Voices raised from the purgatory of youthful torment" should finally be heard. In this way, the narration of and commentary on stories in discussion, which Herder describes as "conversation of minds," becomes the instrument for improving humanity.[17]

How can we explain why telling stories and reflecting on history fell so quickly into disrepute? Hegel's polemic against the contemporary magazines (corresponding to Schiller's earlier attack on the culture of readers' circles) attacks the mass-market literature which had been disseminated since the end of the eighteenth century. Hegel's special target is the attitude of reconciliation in these texts (Kotzebue is the exemplary figure here), because, in his view, mass-market literature remains trapped within a normative framework that has already been outstripped by history. How does Wilhelm Grimm's argumentation relate to this issue? In his case, the argument is not based on a faulty or dubious normative quality. Rather, on the one hand, reflection is utterly rejected as an integral part of narrative, while, on the other, a normative concept of humanity ("human nature and the world in their original force") and of art (as a means of elevation) is set up. Wilhelm Grimm's reception of Kleist is no isolated, accidental reception document; rather it summarizes a tendency that had been effective since the Romantic period and that ought to be investigated in light of the novella poetics of the Schlegel brothers. This is the tendency to dislodge the genre of the novella or tale from the Enlightenment institution of literature.

"Novella Theory"

One of the peculiarities of the study of German literature is that it treats programmatic statements by authors as theory, that is, it treats these statements as something that frames interpretation rather than as the object of historical investigation.[18]

In their programmatic statements, the Schlegel brothers attempt first of all to construct a concept of genre. Historically speaking, they establish the novella as a modern genre that emerges in tandem with the privileging of particular ranks;[19] sociologically speaking, they attribute the novella to the higher ranks where a need for sociable entertainment through conversation [*Unterhaltung*] first emerges. For August Wilhelm Schlegel, Boccaccio offers the model for this genre because his *Decameron* represents the unity of novella narration and "novella theory." The historical-functional significance of Schlegel's generic definition seems in my view to lie in the use of the concept of "entertainment" [*Unterhaltung*]. The concept hangs in suspense between "divertissement" [amusement or diversion] and conversation and may generate a variety of connotations. Those connotations associated with the concept of divertissement recall the feudal courtly institutionalization of literature which the Enlightenment had opposed. On the other hand, this concept excludes certain other connotations: those that take as their point of departure the rational discourse of a literary public sphere. In Goethe's *Unterhaltung deutscher Ausgewanderten* [Entertainment of German emigrants] (1795), entertainment and "sociable" behavior become normative concepts: "There was only one law in society, but that was strictly observed: not to talk specifically about the incidents of the moment and instead to collect all sorts of stories from other periods and countries, which could be collectively enjoyed."

Achim von Arnim's notion of a "winter society in a bad mood" intends, as consistently as Goethe's emigrants repress the French Revolution, to repress the occupation of Berlin by Napoleon's troops.[20] Sociability is interesting primarily as a lifestyle, not as the limit condition for the rational discussion of problems of norms. As telling stories becomes disconnected from rational discourse, sociability becomes the object of the reader's pleasure. Unlike in Diderot's stories, sociability for Goethe and

Arnim is not the result of rational discourse (the product of labor) but a fixed frame as exemplified by the aristocratic salon. The reader enjoys the story and the sociability represented in it as an "extraordinary incident" and a particular lifestyle, respectively.

The reassociation of entertainment with the hierarchical culture of divertissement can also be seen in the traditional lineage presented by the Schlegel brothers. The history of the novella, whose "masters" are said to be Boccaccio, Cervantes, and Goethe, in their view had just passed the period of their apotheosis: it is projected into a past era, "when chivalry, religion, and custom united the nobler part of Europe." The names of Voltaire and Diderot do not appear in this history. We can thus conclude that the Schlegel brothers are concerned to dislodge the tale from the Enlightenment institution of literature and attribute to it, in the form of the novella, an elevated artistic form. This claim can be confirmed by a further observation. The Schlegel brothers' program reveals a normative concept of genre in noticeable contrast to the multiplicity of free narrative forms that had developed during the Enlightenment era. Their argument is surprising, especially in light of their own claim, especially on the part of Friedrich Schlegel, on experimental freedom. The aesthetic norm to which the novella is indebted is the classical concept of symbol. The novella is supposed to "impress [us], on the one hand, by its rare uniqueness and, on the other, by a certain general validity, if it is to be authentic."[21] It ought "to be at home in the real world" but should also "ennoble" that world, although not "unduly."[22] The idealization postulate applied to the novella defines it as an "antidote" to a "thoroughly odious" reality. The motifs should be "common," but they should be organized in such a way that they can be reconciled with the "laws and dispositions of high society," where the novella "has its origin and its home."[23] This is the achievement of the "superior perspective" of the "educated" narrator.[24]

Strictly speaking, it would be one-sided to stress only the normative moment of the Schlegels' novella programmatic and to treat this as an attempt to revoke the Enlightenment's emancipation of narrative from generic obligations and to subject a particular genre, the novella, to the classical idealization postulate. Rather, the reflections of the Schlegel brothers contain distinctly modern moments, such as when they treat prose as the "original and essentially proper form" of the novella or name subjectivity as its distinctive character [Gehalt].[25] Yet, at this point, Friedrich Schlegel introduces a further limitation: subjectivity should be "both indirectly and concretely represented," because this "indirect representation of the subjective can often be more appropriate."[26] The reemployment of feudal-courtly normative conceptions such as the *doctrine classique* and the demand for *bienséance* [decorum] is hard to miss here.

What seems to me more important is another of their reflections:

> Therefore, modern literature should also have a historical genre of its own, whose achievement consists in relating something that finds no place in actual history but is nonetheless of general interest. The object of history is the progressive impact of humankind and will also be what is continually happening, the daily run of the world, which deserves mention. The genre that takes on this task is the novella. . . . The novella is a story out of history; it relates remarkable incidents that have taken place behind the backs of civil constitutions and arrangements.[27]

The definition of the novella as a "historical genre peculiar [to modern literature]" reveals that August Wilhelm Schlegel well knows the tradition from which he would like to dissociate himself: Diderot, whose name does not appear here, also describes his tales as *contes historiques* [historical tales]. Moreover, the formulation in the last sentence recalls Schiller or Meissner and their attempts to write a history of the everyday life of civil [*bürgerlich*] society through the medium of stories that ought to "communicate the experience of actually occurring events."[28] It is rather Friedrich Schlegel who abrogates this connection, in that he dissolves the link between novella and history in a play on words: "[It is the novella]: a story that, strictly speaking, does not belong to history and that gives life to irony from the moment of its birth."[29] The (hi)story that the novella tells is supposed to be only "for itself" and to interest only the "individual." Using irony, it continually cancels the latent link (latent because of its "concrete" mode of representation) between subjectivity and the movement of history. Schlegel's definition of the novella finally envisages constituting the genre as a pure artistic form occasioned by any content whatever.[30]

Detachment

The few examples available of Kleist's own opinions do not allow us to attribute to him particular aesthetic ideas; we do not know what significance he gave to narrative. We have to rely on the stories themselves and the framing conditions within which he published and was received (or not received), in order to establish the functional determination of his narrative. Kleist published his stories first in magazines and then shortly afterward in a volume, *Erzählungen*. As opposed, for example, to the novellas of Ludwig Tieck or Achim von Arnim, which were tied, however loosely, to a frame narrative, Kleist's stories are almost violently detached and self-enclosed single works. The significance of this refusal to frame the stories can be read off a remark of Arnim's. In the *Schlussbericht* [final report] of his *Landhausleben* cycle, the first-person narrator defends himself against the charge that he had rebelled against the mode of observation used in the "Wintergarten": "You should have validated each story by way of its frame of sociable conversation and the criticism offered in that frame." The first-person narrator's argument operates on several levels: on the level of the development of the material (if we do not want to speak of "literary modes"), the rejection of the frame corresponds to the emancipation of narrative from rational discourse and from criticism. On the level of the development of norms, the argument goes in different directions: on the one hand, criticism is simply dismissed as a kind of sickness, which conceals the attack on the Enlightenment; on the other, it is reduced to the judgment of the *aesthetic value* of individual stories. In this framework, criticism emerges as a response to individual possibilities for decision, as the curtailment of the reader's aesthetic competence:

> I reply: "Experience has taught me that these social interjections are ignored or skipped by most readers, because they are nothing more than fragments of an ongoing story. Critical judgment of the stories, on the other hand, appears to be completely misconceived because every reader, when faced with this unfortunate criticism, will prefer to go his own way, resisting foreign constraints. If he still remains free from this unseemliness, he must abhor this kind of judgment of his life as an intrusion into the right to a free existence.[31]

The timeliness of Arnim's defense is revealed in Wilhelm Grimm's reaction to *Landhausleben*. Using arguments based on the aesthetic of autonomy, he criticizes individual stories for diversity of elements in them. According to Grimm, Arnim neglects the strict separation between novella and account, between narrative and rational discourse. Grimm's point of departure is the contemporary reader, who responds to the material with certain presuppositions, wanting either art or something quite different, such as philosophy or science. "Whoever reads [novellas] does [not] want his pleasure disturbed by commentary that he does not really understand. In my opinion, poetry itself may complain that you have put more on to her shoulders than she can or ought to bear."[32] Clearly the educated bourgeois reader's reception attitude toward the Enlightenment institution of literature has radically changed. Grimm assumes that the reader is no longer capable of developing anything other than a "purely aesthetic" interest in the material, or treating the aesthetic object as an occasion for reflection.

For Grimm, the split in the reading public between an educated elite and culture consumers is a sort of "natural" occurrence. It does not represent a problem for him. To reformulate this literary sociological "fact" as a problem, I would begin with a form of distribution that was altogether successful in this period: chrestomathy or anthologization. What is the significance of the appearance, at the beginning of the nineteenth century up to 1825, of successive editions of anthologies of selected passages from Jean Paul's work? Pölitz, the well-known publisher, justified his enterprise in the following way:

> The striking and beautiful elements in his writings stand apart from the context in which they appear to such a degree that they can be presented separately. This separation can therefore be profitably undertaken. No writer of the current period uses so many maxims so often as Jean Paul does. But, in the context of an integral literary work, they are not so thoroughly absorbed and not so striking as when they are collected and put together to form a new whole. In this assembly . . . a collection is constructed that can guarantee pure, lasting, and satisfying pleasure, since it excludes so much that is overwrought, mystical, half-true and derived from a one-sided view of the objects at hand.[33]

Jean Paul presents a problem for a conception of literature grounded in the aesthetic of autonomy: his novels can only with difficulty be subsumed under the category of organic whole. The idea that one could, without interfering with their form, see them as examples of a nonautonomous, nonorganic conception of literature does not occur to his contemporaries trapped in the idealist aesthetic. At the same time, however, Jean Paul was such a popular writer precisely because, in contrast to the autonomous, "high" literature of the period, he challenged the normative orientation of his contemporaries—with maxims. What emerges here is a remarkably odd image. Anthology extracts were drawn from the individual works of Jean Paul, cleansed of nonorganic and morally or politically unreliable moments; these extracts were nonetheless supposed to suggest the harmonious wholeness of the work, although the selection was in fact determined by moral-practical interests (as a "beneficial" book). We can see first of all the possibility of an alternative conception of literature emerging here which treats the work not as a detached totality but as a medium of present-day reflection.[34] We can also see that the work itself is robbed of its critical content and pressed into service for the dominant conceptions of norm and value.[35]

The example of the Jean Paul chrestomathy should explain why readers' needs for normative orientation and meaning, which were not answered by autonomous ("high") literature, were falsely satisfied by way of the instrumentalization of individual works.[36] Insofar as the material conditions for the dissemination of a critical public sphere disappear, there is a growing danger that the attachment to Enlightenment-bourgeois conceptions of literature appears to be repressive or overtaken by an expanding mass-market literature.

This material enables us to explain what one might call the "solipsism" of the Kleistian novella. We know from a letter from Clemens Brentano that Kleist wrote stories only reluctantly and because of material need, and that this compromise with the demands of the literary market "infinitely humiliated him."[37] Kleist feared being branded as trivial and with good reason. For, despite the patronage of Adam Heinrich Müller, esteemed by the elegant and educated society of Dresden, the problem was not only the failure of the project of the magazine *Phoebus* but also the fact that society judged Kleist's stories as "flat." Perceived as "reminiscences of Iffland," the stories were excluded from the realm of "high art." Müller explicitly defended the publication of the stories in an *art magazine* against Friedrich von Gentz, who was not quite qualified in artistic matters. This defense is interesting because it bears witness to contemporary uncertainty about the function of literature. Müller attributes artistic character to Kleist's stories, although their content spills over into the moral realm. His justification is the idealization postulate of the aesthetic of autonomy. Kleist's novellas belong to the realm of art not only "because of the unparalleled art of the representation" but also because of their "moral elevation" and "royal truth" (as against the common, the natural, or characteristic of the rabble).[38]

As a title for a volume of stories, Kleist first suggested "Moralische Erzählungen" to his publisher but later abandoned this allusion to Cervantes.[39] The unadorned title, *Erzählungen*, which he ends up with, gives us an indication of his intention. He does not want to compete with the *Moralische Erzählungen* of the "favored" August Lafontaine, to whom August Wilhelm Schlegel had dedicated one of his polemical reviews but, rather, wants to compel the acceptance of the tale in the domain of "high literature."[40] Kleist thus offers a radical response to the dichotomization that splits German culture into autonomous art for the few and entertainment for the many; we might ask whether the price for the legitimation of the story is [too] high. Kleist destroys that connection between narrative and rational discourse which had constituted the Enlightenment institution of literature. His stories repudiate the recipient as participating and judging dialogue partner. Kleist abandons the attempt to address determinate recipients, that is, those that can be sociohistorically located, or to allow them to appear in the frame of the novella, as was the case with Diderot and also with Arnim and Tieck. The same process of developing the material, whereby the novella emerges as a "pure" art form, removes it from public debate.[41]

The aporia in this answer may be clarified with reference to Georg Lukács's early *Heidelberger Ästhetik*, which represents one of the most radical formulations of the aesthetic of autonomy and thus marks the moment in which this aesthetic turns into aestheticism:

In the aesthetic, the attention is focused on a singular and incomparable object separated out from every context, medium, or sphere. . . . In this light, the process of creation appears to be a remarkable combination of activity and contemplation, an activity which attempts to construct a subjective-metaphysical object world for contemplation (Vision) as a self-enclosed totality (the work). This act is always directed toward a completely detached work. . . . The recipient then may realize aesthetic conduct only in his or her experience if she or he confronts that object as the only real thing; if the mere thought of the possibility of another object arises, which must necessarily happen, if the possibility of a context, in which this object occurs or within which it can be placed, is understood, then immanence to experience is abandoned. . . . The immanence called for here is so strong that the "excluded" reality receives not a single polemical mention.[42]

The confrontation, suggested here, between a narrative work from the beginning of the nineteenth century and aesthetic theory from the beginning of the twentieth allows us to undertake the construction of a tradition. Lukács describes the aesthetic treatment of production and reception as a radical detachment of the aesthetic object. This detachment can indeed be seen as the fundamental principle of Kleistian narrative. Without a frame, the novellas are presented to an anonymous recipient, whom they confront as isolated works of art. Furthermore, Kleist isolates a single incident within each story. The isolation of the incident seems to me more than an internal aesthetic procedure. Kleist scholarship has repeatedly drawn attention to the situation, the accidental occurrence, as the central problem of Kleistian narrative. And it has also been noted that detached, single events are juxtaposed without connection in the novellas. This narrative discontinuity is nonetheless solved, by means of a double insurance. First, the solution is attributed to "artistic law," then established on the level of syntax (with the famous Kleistian conjunction "so . . . that" [*dergestalt . . . dass*]) and brought together under the rubric of an "I" understood as an experiential totality.[43]

If we take this moment of discontinuity seriously, however, the detachment of the event can be understood as a means that enables Kleist to treat the novella as an autonomous work of art. But the often violent character of this detachment also bears witness to the producer's profound uncertainty about the possible triviality of his story, the interest of which would then lie in a series of various stimuli provoked by horror effects. The citation from Lukács's early aesthetics demonstrates the danger of artistic autonomy: its conversion to aestheticism. The concept of "immanence to experience," as Lukács employs it, in fact reduces the reception of the individual work (which has to be stripped of all possible links to reality) to a momentary stimulus and response. In this way, the autonomous work is unwittingly pulled in the direction of light fiction, which, in the terms of traditional theories of evaluation, is characterized as "appropriate attitude that is carried by mood and focused on the I."[44] The ambivalent relationship in Kleistian narrative between a radicalized autonomy of art and triviality (itself characteristic of certain aestheticist works) makes possible the poststructuralist reading of Mathieu Carrière:

> [Kleist's] genius, his secret plan of action, consists in having invented and shaped linguistic techniques that transform every feeling, every position of desire into affect-machines. . . . the language that still speaks here is full of violence, cruelty, and grace. Affect is the mysterious object of the beginning or the end: affect as insignificant, nonsubjective unity that circulates among agencies and provides them with energy. . . . To make affect circulate entails producing unconscious desires, and the most abstract, most effective, most secret machines would be those which set in motion the strings of history itself. Beings, characters, become marionettes, gauche or graceful, according to the intrusions from the pure "outside."[45]

What concerns me here is not to criticize particular elements of poststructuralist thought in this interpretation but rather the issue of tradition construction. The aestheticist-poststructuralist reading turns Kleist retroactively into an author of light fiction by translating the "horrible" into the secret truth of a narrative uncoupled from the consciousness of a producing subject, or into the "electrical tension" which the isolated events load onto the affect-machine.[46] What is telling here are the stereotypical moments of stimulation of the *l'art pour l'art* text: love and death, nomad and marionette, horror and lust, free-floating affects as stimuli for the connoisseur recipient.

Interpretation and Evaluation

Das Erdbeben in Chili [The earthquake in Chile], like all of Kleist's stories, has been interpreted so often that, even outside the frame of institutional research, the conclusion has been reached that interpretation can well come to an end. The question of how the individual work is to be treated seems fair to me. The foregoing reflections should have made clear that ideology critique has a place here. In this context, I would prefer to leave a systematic analysis of concepts such as "contemporaneity," "historicity," "application," and concentrate instead on a number of practical problems. If the object of our investigation were a romantic fairy tale, such as Tieck's *Blond Egbert*, we could examine it as a stage in a particular development of artistic material. My methodological points of departure are as follows: (1) the historical estimation of an individual work can be accomplished only when one takes into account the state of the artistic material to which the work refers (in this case: the reworking of a folktale); and, (2) deviations from the selected artistic material (transformation of given motifs or forms, for example) can be understood as an index of a textual intention that can be reconstructed. We might then ask about the historical content in the reworking and actualization of myth against the rebellious rationality of the folktale: is this a romantic flight from reality or a hidden critique of classical ideality, in which the tragic side of the historical process is expressed, even if the critique of suffering is limited to one's own individuality?[47]

In the case of *Erdbeben in Chili*, our point of departure is the fact that there is a whole series of stories which are adaptations of this one (as with other novellas by Kleist).[48] These adaptations are in no way different from thousands of other stories in a "criminal" or "fateful" or "sensational" vein. Only when published in "consumer" form in large circulation recreational magazines "did these stories become available in affordable form for a larger circle of readers."[49] This kind of publication leads to the question of the difference between adaptation and original; that resembles the question of formulating the difference between work of art and mass-market product but grounds the problem of evaluation in proof of the "literariness" or triviality of the text. This formulation is that of Wolfgang Kayser, for example, who finds Kleist's proximity to the narrative literature of his contemporaries, especially the horror literature, disturbing. He would prefer to reassure himself of the distance between Kleistian narrative and the mass-market literature by making the former itself the "object of contemplation."[50]

It is not easy to resist being seduced by the aura of the (canonized) work. We need an evaluative criterion that can function independently of aesthetic or stylistic questions (and thus independently of our prejudices about the art or style of an author) but not independently of the question of form. The value of the individual work for a discussion of social norms could be such a criterion. This criterion seems to me implicit in some recent interpretations of *Erdbeben in Chili*, which get beyond the traditional idea of the novella based on Goethe's generic foundation in the opposition: chaos/passion/freedom versus order/restriction/law.[51] In his convincing attempt at a progressive interpretation of Kleist, which is linked to the historicophilosophical reflections of *Dialectic of Enlightenment*, Peter Horn elaborates the anarchic moment of the novella. In his view, the earthquake is not a blind natural disaster but rather a sort of historical experiment that reveals what lies behind the facade of "legitimate statehood [*Rechtstaatlichkeit*] according to Rousseau, human nature deformed and corrupted by socialization."[52] In this light, the famous scene of the reunited lovers' brief moment of happiness, that "beautiful night" which they experience "as though it were the garden of Eden" (15) becomes the central demonstration of Kleist's anarchism. It ought to show "that human beings may live [and so realize themselves] without domination, that is, in anarchy, but not without community."[53]

This attempt to render a story contemporary is rightly distinct from a political critique based on the personal position of the author of that story. We may recall Lukács's reception of Kleist, in which he calls Kleist a "mistaken old-Prussian *Junker*."[54] Is the critique plausible? In a recent study of the history of the *Berliner Abendblätter*, Dirk Grathoff gives a detailed analysis of Kleist's political position which attempts to counter the thesis of a reactionary Kleist corresponding to the world of the Christian German society, but does not provide a point of reference for as wide-ranging an interpretation of Kleist's political views as Peter Horn's.[55] According to Grathoff, Kleist is a liberal who represented a position independent of state and government interests and allowed both defenders and detractors (including reactionaries such as A. H. Müller) of the Stein-Hardenberg reforms to publish in his newspaper. Kleist's call for a "liberal order of things" would then correspond to that in a political public sphere.[56]

In order to supplement Horn's progressive reading in an ideological-critical fashion, I do not want to focus on Kleist's political views, but rather on the *form* of the novel. As I have argued, the fundamental principle of the form is its detachment and discontinuity. We can get a sense of the distinctiveness of Kleistian narrative if we pay attention to what is excluded in the adaptations. In the adaptation, the entire middle section is missing, with its idyll, which is also an indication of a human community that breaks the bounds of a hierarchical society. All that is communicated is what is necessary for the development of the plot (that Josephe kills Don Fernando's child). What is also lacking is the detailed description of the human suffering as a result of the natural disaster as well as the acts of atrocity committed by the riotous mob at the end of the story, when the viewer's gaze is forced to dwell on the murder of a victim of lynch-justice painted in all its baroque (or almanac-like) grisliness. It is precisely at this moment that Kleist's otherwise rapidly and briskly reporting narrator appears to bring the story to a halt.[57] Kleistian narrative seems to me to run the risk of fragmenting into single moments that are not connected to one another.[58] This impression corresponds to that of the first recipients, especially those who were close to Kleist: "The close delineation of his figures and relationships becomes *mannered,* against which he tosses the secret as secret so as to give the fearful reality a counterweight. Since he leaves this secret unresolved, the context and the reader's feelings remain disturbed.[59]

"The reader's feelings" remain "disturbed" because she or he cannot establish a connection between the images of horror at the beginning and end of the story and the idyll in the middle. Nature and society confront the viewer as images of torment or blessedness, to be enjoyed as isolated, detached images, without any connection to the real world. "Every one of his paths will lead to the edge of the great abyss and will not be able to remain still anywhere except at the edge of that abyss. And the deepest meaning of the forms is this: to lead to the great moment of profound speechlessness and the aimless motley of life so constructed as though it hastens along only for the sake of such moments."[60] Meeting in this concentration on the gaze into the abyss are the legend, mass-market horror stories, and aestheticism. The legend unfolds to pull the gaze of the audience to the images of horror which it presents as warning signs, showing human beings at the mercy of nature and domination what sort of punishment threatens them if they dare to transgress the bounds of the law. Just as in the legend the shepherds look back in spite of the warning to *see* how the puppets, which they themselves put together and blasphemously baptized, come alive, flay their comrades, and then spread the bloody skin on the roof of the hut, so we look at the horrible images in Kleist's stories, images that are unfamiliar but somehow awaited: Kleist's novellas take part in the myth of prohibition.[61]

In a study of the nineteenth-century horror story, Jörg Schönert argues in terms of the immanent evolution of the textual material in describing the functional transformation of the horror story. According to him, the collective experience of fear was mediated by horror and resolved in critical reflection so that deviation could be understood as a functional part of human practice. In "romantic horror," an individual figure becomes the bearer of this fear: "The resultant loss of collective identification is nonetheless balanced by the specific and sustained experience of fear, . . . by 'thickened experience.' "[62] The objectivist mode of consideration does not help us answer the question how we might judge a narrative which delivers its recipient to a prohibition similar to that in the legend.[63]

I do not wish to be misunderstood: the reference to the legend does not entail associating Kleist's stories with the genre of "novella of fate" (H. Pong). I am afraid, rather, that Mathieu Carrière strikes the right note when he appropriates Deleuze and Guattari to speak of an affect-machine in his representation of Kleist's work: "Thus, a book no longer has an object. . . . One never asks what a book is intended to mean. . . . instead one asks how a book functions, in which directions it allows for the flow of intensities, into which multiplicities it introduces and transforms its own multiplicity."[64] The price that Kleist pays to force an acknowledgment of his stories as works of art seems to me to be their separation from the debate of social norms; we inquire not so much after the significance of his novellas as after their formal functional mechanism. The textually imma-nent classification of these novellas that argues for their artistic character rightly claims that Kleist "relates incidents and nothing else" and "makes the opacity of *all* reality visible by way of a rigorously artistic architec-tonic," and that "he thus radically [transcends] the notion of the novella as a form of sociable entertainment."[65] Yet, one ought to make this "descrip-tion" the point of departure for the critique of the evolution of textual material.

Notes

1. René Wellek and Austin Warren, *Theory of Literature* (New York: Harcourt, Brace, 1949), 120.
2. For methodological parameters of the following remarks, see Peter Bürger, "The Institution of Art as a Category of the Sociology of Literature," in this volume.
3. See *Aufklärung und literarische Öffentlichkeit* ed. Christa Bürger, Peter Bürger, and Jochen Schulte-Sasse (Frankfurt, 1980), passim.
4. Quoted in H. Sembdner, ed., *Heinrich von Kleists Lebensspuren* (Frankfurt, 1977), 305f.
5. See Peter Bürger, *Zur Kritik der idealistischen Ästhetik* (Frankfurt, 1983), chap. 3.
6. Quoted by Sembdner, *Kleists Lebensspuren*, 305f. See also K. A. Varnhagen

von Ense's discussion of Arnim's novella collection of 1812 in his *Literaturkritiken*, ed. K. F. Gille (Tübingen, 1977), 4f.

7. Sembdner, *Kleists Lebensspuren*, 307.
8. Hermann Broch, "Methodisch konstruirt," in his *Die Schuldlosen* (Munich, 1965), 58.
9. G. W. F. Hegel, "Wer denkt abstrakt?" in his *Werke*, ed. E. Moldenhauer and K. M. Michel (Frankfurt, 1970), 2:578.
10. Ibid., 579.
11. Schiller, "Merkwürdige Rechtsfälle als ein Beitrag zur Geschichte der Menschheit," in his *Sämtliche Werke*, ed. G. Fricke and H. G. Göpfert (Munich, 1967), 5:864f.
12. A. G. Meissner, "Skizzen," in *Erzählende Prosa der Goethezeit*, ed. B. M. Beaujean (Hildesheim, 1979), 1:29ff., emphasis added. The editor's judgment of Meissner is significant in this context: "Like most of the mediocre talents of this period, he remained trapped within the parameters of the Enlightenment" (513).
13. Ibid., 30.
14. Achim von Arnim, "Der Wintergarten," in his *Sämtliche Romane und Erzählungen*, ed. W. Migge (Munich, 1963), 303f.
15. See L. Rohmer, *Kalendergeschichten und Kalendar* (Wiesbaden, 1978), 46ff., 85.
16. Johann Herder, "Adrastea," in his *Sämtliche Werke*, ed. B. Suphan (Berlin, 1885), 23:224.
17. Herder, "Adrastea," 228f., 238. See O. Frels, "Der Literaturbegriff des späten Herder. Eine Studie zur Kritik der Autonomie-aesthetik um 1800," (Ph.D. diss., University of Bremen, 1981).
18. See J. Kunz's introduction to J. Kunz, ed., *Novelle* (Darmstadt, 1968).
19. Friedrich Schlegel, "Nachricht von den poetischen Werken des Johannes Boccaccio (1801)," in Kunz, *Novelle*, 43.
20. Arnim, "Der Wintergarten," 132, 137.
21. August Wilhelm Schlegel, "Vorlesungen," in Kunz, *Novelle*, 45.
22. Ibid., 49.
23. F. Schlegel, "Nachricht," 41.
24. A. W. Schlegel, "Vorlesungen," 49.
25. Ibid., 45; F. Schlegel, "Nachricht," 41.
26. F. Schelegel, "Nachricht," 40f.
27. A. W. Schlegel, "Vorlesungen," 44f. and 50.
28. Ibid., 45.
29. F. Schlegel, "Nachricht," 41.
30. Ibid., 41f.
31. Arnim, "Landhausleben," in his *Sämtliche Romane und Erzählungen* 3:518f.

32. W. Grimm to Arnim, 20 September 1827, quoted in Arnim, *Sämtliche Romane und Erzählungen* 3:795.

33. C. H. L. Pölitz, *Jean Pauls Geist oder Chrestomathie der vorzüglichsten, kräftigsten und gelungensten Stellen aus seinen sämtlichen Schriften*, quoted in H. Verschuren, *Jean Pauls "Hesperus" und das zeitgenössische Lesepublikum* (Assen, 1980), 83.

34. For example, Caroline Herder reads Jean Paul in this way when she treats "single images" in the novels as "materials of the current period," which can be connected to the life world of the novel's subjects; see her letter to Jean Paul of 26 June 1797, quoted in Verschuren, *Jean Pauls "Hesperus,"* 48. Her comparison between the novels of Jean Paul and those of Münster does not envisage the organic unity of the work of art but, rather, the recipient's capacity for assimilating single moments in the work in practical life.

35. See Burkhardt Lindner, "Das Opfer der Poesie. Zur Konstellation von Aufklärungsroman und Kunstautonomie am Ende des 18. Jahrhunderts," in Bürger, Bürger, and Schulte-Sasse, *Aufklärung und literarische Öffentlichkeit*, 294ff.

36. On the problem of dichotomy, see *Zur Dichotomisierung von hoher und niederer Literatur*, ed. Christa Bürger, Peter Bürger, and Jochen Schulte-Sasse (Frankfurt, 1982).

37. Clemens Brentano to Achim von Arnim, 1 December 1811, quoted in Heinrich von Kleist, *Sämtliche Werke und Briefe*, ed. H. Sembdner (Munich, 1964), 2:895.

38. Adam Heinrich Müller to Gentz, March 1808, quoted in Sembdner, *Kleists Lebensspuren*, 212.

39. Ibid.

40. See A. W. Schlegel, "Mode-Roman Lafontaine," in his *Sämtliche Werke*, ed. E. Böcking (Leipzig, 1846–47), vol. 12.

41. We might say that this development makes traditional German literature studies' preference for the novella comprehensible.

42. Georg Lukács, *Heidelberger Ästhetik* (1916–18), vol. 17 of *Werke*, ed. Georg Markus and F. Bensler (Darmstadt, 1974), 107ff.

43. "Poetically coming to terms [*Bewältigung*] with reality means nothing more than: . . . concretely realizing a randomly determined reality as a linguistic medium and thus organizing this reality in an overarching context. The antinomies of the situation, accident and unity, are thus absorbed into the linguistic structure of poetry" (Hans-Peter Hermann, "Zufall und Ich. Zum Begriff der Situation in den Novellen Heinrich von Kleists," *Germanistische-Romanistische Monatsschrift*, n.s. 11 [1961]: 97 and passim).

44. Jochen Schulte-Sasse, *Literarische Wertung* (Stuttgart, 1976), 8.

45. Mathieu Carrière, *Für eine Literatur des Krieges: Kleist* (Basel, 1981), 117f.

46. Ibid., 21.

47. See Christa Bürger, *Tradition und Subjectivität* (Frankfurt, 1980), 149.

48. The more insignificant the changes become that Kleist made in the magazine versions of his stories when preparing them for publication in book form, the more striking this fact should be for a stylistically informed literary scholarship. See K. Kanzog, *Prolegomena zu einer historisch-kritischen Ausgabe der Werke Heinrich von Kleists* (Munich, 1970).

49. See A. Estermann, "Nacherzählungen Kleistscher Prosa," in K. Kanzog, ed., *Text und Kontext* (Berlin, 1979), 81.

50. Wolfgang Kayser, "Kleist als Erzähler," in W. Müller-Seidel, ed. *Heinrich von Kleist. Aufsätze und Essays* (Darmstadt, 1967), 230.

51. See Goethe's well-known expression in the *Wahlverwandschaften* (Elective affinities), in which he speaks of "the conflict between the lawful and the outlaw"; cited by Kunz, *Novellen*, 33.

52. Peter Horn, *Heinrich von Kleists Erzählungen. Eine Einführung* (Königstein, 1978), 114.

53. Ibid., 128.

54. Georg Lukács, *Deutsche Realisten des 19. Jahrhunderts* (Berlin/DDR: 1952), 22.

55. Dirk Grathoff, "Die Zensurkonflickte der *Berliner Abendblätter*," in K. Peter et al., *Ideologiekritische Studien zur Literatur* (Frankfurt, 1972), 152.

56. "Kleist's turn to a larger public was certainly politically motivated insofar as . . . he was aware of the political significance of the press and wanted to contribute to better information and thus to the political consciousness and mobilization of the 'people' [*Volk*]. This moment has a progressive significance because it was directed against the absolutist politics of 'managing the people' in Prussia" (ibid., 152).

57. This claim contradicts the thesis of H. H. Holz, for whom Kleist's turn to a "factual narrative style" represents the attempt to "wrest the guarantee of truth within the horizon of the failing articulation of language" (*Macht und Ohnmacht der Sprache* [Frankfurt, 1962], 149).

58. If we assume that Grathoff's analysis does not simply read Habermas's category of *public sphere* [*Öffentlichkeit*] into Kleist's journalistic activities, and that his claim that Kleist is concerned to construct a rational public sphere is plausible, then we might conclude that his literary work can be divided into a part that is open to the public sphere and a part that excludes it.

59. Caroline de la Motte-Fouqué, *Gespräch über die Erzählungen von H. von Kleist* (1812), quoted by H. Sembdner, *Heinrich von Kleists Nachruhm. Eine Wirkungsgeschichte in Dokumente* (Bremen, 1967), 629.

60. Georg Lukács, *Die Seele und die Formen* (Neuwied, 1971), 164f.; trans. Anna Bostock, *Soul and Form* (Cambridge, Mass.: MIT Press, 1974).

61. See *Tradition und Subjektivität*, chap. 10; also see Christa Bürger, "Die soziale Funktion volkstümlicher Erzählformen—Sage und Märchen," in H. Ide, ed., *Kritische Lesen* (Stuttgart, 1971), 26–56.

62. Jörg Schönert, "Behaglicher Schauer und distanzierter Schrecken," in *Literatur in der sozialer Bewegung* (Tübingen, 1977), 52.

63. R. Wilkening's perceptive investigation of perspectivism in Kleist's narrative, which produces similar results to those of Peter Horn's study, tends to use the concepts of reception aesthetics in rather too abstract a fashion, when he claims, for example, "his integrative point of view helps the reader critically to judge the perspectively limited view of characters and narrative" ("Studien zum textinternen Perspektivismus und seiner leseorientierenden Funktion im Erzählen Heinrich von Kleists, dargestellt an der Novelle 'Das Erdbeben von Chili' " [Ph.D. diss., University of Bremen, 1978], 233).

64. Gilles Deleuze and Félix Guattari, *Rhizome* (Paris, 1976), 9.

65. Benno von Wiese, *Novelle* (Stuttgart, 1964), 55.

1. "The Institution of Art as a Category of the Sociology of Literature" is translated from "Institution Kunst als literatursoziologische Kategorie," in *Vermittlung—Rezeption—Funktion: Ästhetische Theorie und Metho-dologie der Literaturwissenschaft*, by Peter Bürger (Frankfurt: Suhrkamp Verlag, 1979), © Suhrkamp Verlag Frankfurt am Main 1979.

2. "The Functional Transformation of Dramatic Literature in the Era of Emergent Absolutism" is translated from "Zum Funktionswandel der dramatischen Literatur in der Epoche des entstehenden Absolutismus," first published in *Französische Literatur in Einzeldarstellung*, vol. 1, edited by Peter Brockmeier and Herman H. Wetzel (Stuttgart: J. B. Metzlersche Verlagsbuchhandlung, 1981), © Peter Bürger 1981.

3. "Problems in the Functional Transformation of Art and Literature during the Transition from Feudal to Bourgeois Society" is translated from "Zum Problem des Funktionswandels von Kunst und Literatur in der Epoche des Übergangs von der feudalen zur bürgerlichen Gesellschaft," first published in *Liliart* 32 (1978), © Peter Bürger 1978.

4. "Human Misery or Heaven on Earth? The Novel between Enlightenment and the Autonomy of Art" is translated from "Das menschliche Elend oder Der Himmel auf Erden?" in *Zur Dichotomisierung von hoher und niederer Literatur*, edited by Christa Bürger, Peter Bürger, and Jochen Schulte-Sasse (Frankfurt: Suhrkamp Verlag, 1982), © Suhrkamp Verlag Frankfurt am Main 1982.

5. "Classical Processes of Dissociation: Goethe's *Iphigenia*" is translated from "Klassische Trennungsprozesse," in *Tradition und Subjektivität*, by Christa Bürger (Frankfurt: Suhrkamp Verlag, 1980), © Suhrkamp Verlag Frankfurt am Main 1980.

6. "In Lieu of an Interpretation: Notes on Kleist's Narrative" is translated from "Statt einer Interpretation: Anmerkungen zu Kleists Erzählungen," in *Position der Literaturwissenschaft* (Atheneum Verlag), © Christa Bürger 1985.